Cooking Beyond Measure

How to Eat Well
without
Formal Recipes

Jean Johnson

76^ave Seventy-Sixth Avenue Press
Portland, Oregon

Seventy-Sixth Avenue Press
3524 NE 76th Avenue
Portland, Oregon 97213

Library of Congress Control Number 2008900629

Johnson, Jean, PhD, 1948—

Cooking beyond measure: how to eat well without formal recipes

Includes index.

Cookery (Vegetables and Fruits)
Cookery (American—History)
Food Habits (United States)

ISBN-13 978-0-9815271-0-9
ISBN-10 0-9815271-0-8

Printed in China

For people

too busy to do

the equivalent of small chemistry experiments

when

all they want is

good food.

Acknowledgments

First, to the great scratch cooks in my family: my mother especially, Kathleen Brown Johnson; my aunt, Kirsten Johnson Wilson; and my grandmothers, Carolyn Brown Winandy and Brita Bjornevald Johnson. Second, to the Sixties counterculture for its appetite for change. Lastly, to professors in the Department of History at Washington State University who helped open the windows on my mind.

And for those more immediately involved in this work: the Adobe support team for invaluable technical assistance, neighbor Chad Mortensen for his Canadian generosity in designing the web site, Marsha Buzan for common sense encouragement and love of my stories, Bob Goforth for sustained interest from the beginning when the blog started, Carole Branom for reading a late draft, Olive Blackwell for steadfast enthusiasm, Rick Wagner for coming up with the title, Chris Leck for mighty help on the camera learning curve, John Rupp for early thoughts on the introduction, Laura Berg for latter thoughts on the introduction and her gardener's heart, Rula Awwad-Rafferty for her cook's soul, Michelle Loggins for asking reasonable questions, Robert Olsen for being a pal as the project came to a close, and Dorothy Read who listened attentively and appreciatively to my final read of the manuscript.

Also to Gary and Argelis Lewis for still being around, Matt Loggins for never having left, Doug and Sandy Kypfer for being in the wings, McKee for wherever it is that he is, and the ever-generous late Laurabelle Nelson who, when those inevitable days of second-guessing came, said, "Oh, Jeannie, don't ever give up!"

Table of Contents

Introduction   8

Chapter 1
    Breakfasts   15

Chapter 2
    Starters and Sides   57

Chapter 3
    Soups   89

Chapter 4
    Salads   113

Chapter 5
    Main Dishes   145

Chapter 6
    Endings   183

Index   199

Introduction

I still remember the day at Washington State University when Professor LeRoy Ashby pushed back the sleeves on his sweater as if ready to whip up an omelet. "Most Americans didn't have measuring utensils until the 1900s and 1910s," he said, with an owlish look through his glasses. "These kitchen tools were an outgrowth of the movement called domestic science. It emerged during the late-1890s when the country was industrializing."

Ashby went on to explain that the era was one in which Americans believed fervently in the ability of science and technology to cure our every ill, including less than inspired dinners. "What?" I thought more naively than I should have as a doctoral candidate in US history. "We didn't *always* have measuring cups?"

Stunned as I was, this information simmered on the back burner for years. Indeed, it's notable that when determining a dissertation topic, I consulted my father, not my mother. "What should I do, Dad? Health food or the salmon?" My meat and potatoes father who was born and raised in the Pacific Northwest replied as expected. "Better do the salmon."

Off I went and through dogged persistence if not inspiration, wound up my PhD. All the while, my interest in healthy eating and great cooking never flagged, and years later when I discovered the established field of culinary history, the seed that Ashby planted began to grow.

It didn't take long to find Laura Shapiro's work, and in *Perfection Salad* there the message was again, front and center: Only after the country started engineering and industrializing and building railroads and factories, did we get measuring cups and spoons and begin following precise ingredient-specific recipes.

Shapiro supplies the details on how in the late-1800s Boston elites who had a belly full of the food their Irish help was dishing up, organized training at a school of cooking directed by Fannie Farmer. From her post, this efficient woman wrote the recipe book we now call the *Fannie Farmer Cookbook*, in the process earning herself the title of "the mother of level measurements." As Shapiro writes, "exhaustive precision was not a burden to Miss Farmer, but means to speedy and assured results."

Fine and dandy for that era and the Bostonians, but fast forward a hundred years to our time. We are in the middle of an obesity and overweight epidemic that the federal government has branded a major public health crisis. The economy is also in trouble with our food bills rising faster than our paychecks. Still many of us don't cook and instead head off to groceries and restaurants over and again to buy ready-to-eat food. Why?

We like the taste is one obvious answer. We don't like a mess in the kitchen is another. Then again, many of us feel too tired, too busy to cook.

After all, wasn't that part of what the women's movement was about? Freeing ourselves from the endless, thankless chore of cooking? Perhaps, but few would argue that our current behaviors around food are working for us.

"The truth is that I feel guilty about eating out so much," said Julie Fast, author in Portland, Oregon. "All that salty, greasy, sugary food that I know isn't good for me. I worry about my weight and health, and I would rather save my money for things I really want to do. Somehow, though, it doesn't happen. I live alone, and it's just easier to come to the pub."

Indeed, our physicians and bankers tell us we're living too high on the hog. Yet, we seem caught in a trap that won't let us go. Could it be because the trap has been with us so long we assume it's a vital part of our culinary landscape? Could the trap be the idea that we have come to assume cooking is supposed to be a technical exercise?

Clearly measured recipes with their lists of precise ingredients are great when making a particular pastry or special occasion meals. And many talented scratch cooks consult recipe books for ideas, technique, and theory.

But on a daily basis when all we want is dinner, few of us are up to doing the equivalent of small chemistry experiments. All that one-half cup diced this and that… Besides, more often than not, we don't have all the ingredients the recipe calls for in the house. No wonder the food industry has found it so easy to sell us its products.

Yet, at some level deep in our collective unconscious, could it be that we have resisted becoming mere direction-followers and letting whoever makes up the recipes in cookbooks have all the fun? Indeed, common sense tells us that the amounts prescribed in measured recipes are open to considerable interpretation.

I suggest that we grieve over the loss of the artistry that was once ours in the kitchen. As Richard Olney, the late food and wine critic who loved France so much he moved there, writes in *Lulu's Provencal Table* (1994):

> I often feel guilty when writing recipes. To capture what one can of elusive, changing experience—a fabric of habit, intuition, and inspiration of the moment—and imprison it in a chilly formula composed of cups, tablespoons, inches, and oven temperatures, is like robbing a bird of flight.
> Lulu doesn't measure. When describing liquid quantity, she speaks in terms of ladles, but of course, she doesn't count out ladlefuls—she simply pours in liquid until it looks about right.

France. Thailand. Mexico. Jordan. Everyday home cooks across the globe still revel in the joy and pride that comes from the creative art of cooking. Case in point, a balmy evening in Puebla in 2007. There were six of us writers from *El Norte* with as many Mexican officials, eating mole poblano, turkey smothered in a spicy redolent sauce.

"Puebla is considered a culinary center of Mexico," the state's minister of tourism, Germán Ruiz, told us. "We're known for our mole poblano, and to help keep that tradition alive we have a competition each summer with all the ladies from this area."

"Are the recipes written down somewhere?" a Canadian food writer in our party asked. "Well," said Ruiz, shrugging his very Latin shoulders and lifting a shot of tequila to his lips, "You could write them down, but in the end it's the way you do it. No?"

It was the same when I visited Doug and Sandy Kypfer in Thailand and spent as much time in the kitchen with their Thai cook, Daeng Arporn Punlert, as I did with my expatriate pals. Day after day, Punlert turned out one intoxicatingly flavorful dish after another without cracking a recipe book or using measuring cups and spoons.

Now that I think back, it was much the theme in my mother's kitchen, where I watched her make so many good things, among them the Caesar salad her sons and husband dearly loved. The sumptuous treat depended on her spotting nice looking romaine at the grocery— and being in the mood. She'd get her greens washed and chilled before she left for her job and come dinner time she'd work her magic, no recipe card in sight.

If you figure one generation for every twenty years, there have been around five since Fannie Farmer's influential work fanned from Boston out across the continent in the late-1800s and early-1900s. It's really not that long a time span in the larger scheme of things. Not long enough for us to have completely forgotten how so many of our great, great, greats used to simmer and season and put by and make do in the most splendidly delicious fashion.

That's what this book is devoted to, then. Helping us busy moderns reconnect with the true pleasure of cooking. Encouraging weeknight cooks to leave their measuring cups in the drawer and use what's on hand to make meals from fresh, sustainably grown vegetables and fruits. Meals that are mostly ready in a half hour and are healthy, affordable, and fabulous.

As our beloved grande dame, Julia Child, writes in her magnum opus, *The Way to Cook*, "Even if you're working all day, why buy Chinese takeout, or frozen dinners, or eat at a fast food joint when you can make a fresh, informal home-cooked meal even in a minuscule kitchen—and you will know exactly what you are eating."

So take Alice Waters' delicious revolution a step further. Leave your measuring utensils behind and take back your kitchen. Discover how great food is when it's made freshly with a little creative flair. And how few tricks are needed to send its flavor right over the top.

That's what cooking is about for the world's great ethnic cooks today. That's what it was about for our ancestors just a century ago. And that's what it can again be about for us.

Jean Johnson
Portland, Oregon
11 May 2008

Breakfasts

Breakfast ideas here are for weekdays and weekends. If you're out the door at the crack of dawn and on the McDonald's Egg McMuffin train more than you wished, check out the Egg and Cheese Tacos. Or if you're a granola head at heart, Quinoa Logs might resonate. The logs can even be made the night before or a few days ahead since they are really just a fresh, sugar free granola bar.

For those that have some but not a lot of time for a sit down during the week, there are cereal and fruit ideas as well as pancakes and waffles that can come together surprisingly fast. Pancakes, like Corncakes with Pepper Jack, especially, are quicker than many realize when you store leftover batter in the fridge and simply freshen it as needed.

For more leisurely weekends, there are Rolled Up Pancakes, sure to be a hit around the hacienda—entirely worth the relatively benign learning curve (during which you get to taste plenty of samples). And not to be missed are Bob's Polenta Waffles, golden gems I make when I want a something earthy and good in the soothing colors of the Southwest.

Mainly, though, what you have here is a smattering of suggestions to get your creative sparks going. Once you've accumulated a few things in the pantry and figured out some entirely doable techniques, you'll be able to leave not only fast food train behind, but also those other ready-to-eat products our grocers, coffee shops, and restaurants carry. Before you know it, your wallet will be thicker and your waist thinner.

Breakfasts

Fruit and Cereal
      Figgy Cereal 18
      Cottage Cream 20
      Quinoa with Raspberries and Cashews 22
      Quinoa Logs 25
      Fruit and Dip 28
      Swiss Birkermuesli 29
      Pulled Strawberries 30
      Apples with Beanpaste, Kasha, and Lime 32
      Beanpaste 33
      Thanksgiving Breakfast 34
      KBJ's Cranberries 36
Pancakes and Waffles
      Rolled Up Pancakes 38
      Bob's Polenta Waffles 42
      Corncakes with Pepper Jack 44
Eggs
      Egg and Cheese Tacos 48
      Cheesy Corn Bake 53

Figgy Cereal

Amaranth steams up so white and creamy. Still, it's the fruit in cereal that keeps us coming back to whole grains. Fruit that changes with the seasons. In this case, plump, jammy figs, that my tree Florence tendered even as her leaves were yellowing one glorious autumn, and smooth-skinned kiwis that neighbors Chad Mortensen and Meredith Cairns spied at a u-pick while day tripping in Oregon's wine country.

Recipe Note

Put steamed amaranth in a bowl with flax meal, cottage cream (p. 20), fresh figs, and kiwis. A pinch of cinnamon on top makes figgy amaranth look as scrumptious as it tastes.

Details

Freshly steamed amaranth is wonderful porridge and takes ten to fifteen minutes at a ratio of one part grain to two parts water. Leftovers also revive beautifully simmered in a little water or herb tea.

You can buy expensive flax oil or pre-ground flax meal, but it's so easy to grind your own seeds in the same mill you use for coffee beans. Store delicate flax meal in the fridge. Holistic expert Andrew Weil, MD recommends two tablespoons for a day's requirement of omega-three fatty acids.

Slice the figs crosswise to make fetching tan circlets. They go beautifully with the emerald kiwis. If there are no fresh figs or kiwis in sight, though, whatever fruit's in season is sure to grace amaranth magnificently.

The only sweetener here is cinnamon. Getting acquainted with how ripe fruit tastes when it's not overshadowed by extra sugar or honey is an experience worth investigating.

On Whole Grains and Food Dollars—

Whole grains are right down there on the bottom of the food chain and utterly affordable from bulk bins, even at premium organic prices.

There's amaranth; high protein, fast-cooking quinoa; kasha; millet; and brown rice that has undeservedly "gotten a bad rap," in the words of *New York Times* food writer, Mark Bittman.

This cornucopia of nature's bounty is way more delicious and varied than I ever imagined back in my boxed cereal daze.

Cottage Cream

This concoction is as smooth and splendid as its name. Spooned on breakfast cereals, cottage cream supplies more protein than milk or yogurt.
As the old timers used to say:
It's delicious.
It's nutritious.
It will make you feel ambitious!

No need to limit cottage cream's roll to cereal. If you think of it like yogurt or sour cream, you'll be making this high protein topping for all sorts of things whether you'd like to shed a few pounds or not.

Recipe Note

In the blender add enough milk or water to a carton of cottage cheese to get things whirling. That's it except for flavorings if you want. Vanilla, lemon juice, almond extract. Most anything, even plain, is nice.

Details

The trick to making cottage cream is getting it thick enough, a process helped by a blender with some oomph. Most household blenders have three hundred fifty watts, enough power for smoothies and such but too flabby for thicker blends. I upgraded to five hundred watts without having to go a specialty store. Another approach is to work unplugged and use a spoon to force the cheese through a large sieve, a technique that yields superlative results.

On Making Things Ahead—Cottage cream is an example of a basic you can make ahead when you have a little time. Then when you're hungry, there it is all ready to go with whatever you're dreaming up—like filling the cavity of a butternut squash.

Quinoa with Raspberries and Cashews

It's true that sprouting can seem like quite the project if you've not tried it.

But remember the story about the two armies that were down to nothing but legumes…

The bad guys boiled their beans. The good guys sprouted theirs before they cooked them and with the vibrance they got from this superior nutrition, kept those white hats in place.

When I made this for friend Sandy Kypfer, she said "This is good. You'll have to include it in your cookbook." I think what mainly attracted her were the fresh raspberries we picked out along the back fence, but that's how Plain Jane cooking works. Build a wholesome no frills foundation and then bring on the starlets.

Recipe Note

Spoon leftover quinoa, sprouted wheat berries, and oat bran into cereal bowls. Top with fresh raspberries, pour on unsweetened soy milk, and garnish with raw cashews and a pinch of nutmeg.

Details

Quinoa—leftovers chilled down in the refrigerator—is the mainstay here. Over that scatter enough chewy sprouts and bran to keep things interesting.

Berries and cashews are the ultimate in fast fruit since there is no stopping off at the chopping board.

On Sprouting Grain, Seeds, and Beans—

For breakfasts (cereals, pancakes, and sweet breads), wheat sprouts in earlier than later stages are best because as they don't have the green chlorophyll sprouts acquire as they grow. Whatever the meal, though, sprouted wheat is amazingly welcome stuff—so much so that once people discover the sprouting jar, it gets quite a workout as the oh so sweet and helpful Dulce Del Rio shows.

Mung beans, alfalfa seeds, and wheat berries (kernels of wheat) sprout nicely in a wide mouth quart jar with a circle of screen cut to fit the top and a canning band to hold the screen in place.

Be conservative with your grain, seeds, or beans as they gain considerable volume when they first swell and then send out shoots that mark the beginnings of new life. A nice jar lid full or mound in the palm of your hand is good.

Soak whatever you're sprouting in water overnight. In the morning, drain the liquid and rinse. Keep the jar on its side so the sprouts have room to grow. Continue rinsing daily so they stay fresh. If you're using sprouts in salads or soups, set the jar by a window the last day so light can help develop the chlorophyll.

Quinoa Logs

Necessity is the mother of invention. That's how this delightful breakfast came to be. Friends, Gary and Argelis Lewis, were back in town recording their latest Latin jazz CD, "Prescience." They had to be at the studio early with no time for the table, so I pulled these little logs together for them to take with. Within fifteen minutes Argelis rang. "These are fabulous!" she said, in her Panamanian lilt. "You could get addicted to them!"

Recipe Note

Work nuggets of room temperature caramelized goat cheese (Gjetost) into leftover quinoa and a little flax meal until you have dough that holds together. Form into small logs and roll in cinnamon.

Details

Having a pot of quinoa waiting in the fridge made pulling together this creative, ultrafast meal easy. It also didn't hurt that I'd left a chunk of cheese out from the night before, given our mellow autumn temperatures.

On Sugar Sensitivity—

Although I did nestle these logs in a flat to-go box with some apple chunks, fruit isn't a required component of this breakfast. That's a good thing, according to Karen Seibert, MS, lead nutritionist at Portland's New Seasons markets. "When you eat fruit in the morning it's harder for your body to balance your blood sugar," she explained, "and that can set you up for cravings, especially if you are sensitive to sugar." For those who are sugar sensitive or simply trying to stabilize their blood sugar levels in order to trim off a few pounds, Seibert recommends eating breakfasts high in protein, fat, and fiber—things like frittatas—and leaving fruits until lunch and dinner.

On Caramelized Goat Cheese—

Caramelized goat cheese from Norway, Gjetost (yet-oast), is like savory fudge. Some cheese aficionados including the authoritative Steve Jenkins, say Gjetost is too sweet but I wonder if they've fully explored the wonderful things it does to soup broth and the way it sauces warm salads, not to mention its role in quinoa logs.

Perhaps it's my heritage. Most Norwegian immigrants like my grandparents—Rognald Johnson who skated out across the ice to board the boat and Brita Bjornevald Johnson who entertained sister and fellow travelers on the continental-long railroad trip from Ellis Island—spoke only English to their children to further the melting pot process. Yet, when it came to food it was a different story. Things like lefse, salmon cakes, fattigman, lutefisk, and Gjetost never left the larder for long. That's why mainstream grocers in towns like Portland, Oregon, where so many Scandinavians settled, have carried Gjetost forever.

Tawny, mouth watering Gjetost is also available at whole foods groceries and in cheese shops throughout the country. There's really nothing like caramelized goat cheese.

Fruit and Dip

It's sad when your beautiful fruit gets lost in the cereal bowl under a billows of yogurt or cottage cream. Here's a way to keep things looking fabulous right to the last bite. If you're thinking chip and dip, bingo.

Recipe Note

Put a dollop of cottage cream or yogurt in the center of a breakfast plate and edge with homemade birkermuesli. Arrange chunks of fresh fruit like pulled strawberries (p. 30) over the cereal. Drizzle with the juice from half a lemon. Garnish with a pinch of cinnamon and if you're feeling like exploring the sweet-spicy world of chutneys, a bit of coriander and cayenne as well.

Details

Fresh lemon juice makes fruit and cereal positively shimmer with flavor.

The idea of mixing coriander and cayenne with fruit may seem strange at first but it's common practice in Asia. See if you don't agree that the pair lends a compelling note of intrigue.

Swiss Birkermuesli

Recipe Note

Mix one part rolled oats with half parts wheat germ, oat bran, and flax meal. That's the basic cereal which you can enjoy with fresh fruit. Or if you want something mixed up ahead of time and ready to go, try adding raisins and walnuts, dates and almonds, or dried peaches and pecans for a Southern twist. Store your muesli in the refrigerator to keep the flax meal and wheat germ fresh.

Birkermuesli Backgrounder—Granola is one of those quintessential health food items. It's endured since members of the counterculture first began toasting their own back in the late-1960s. But does a mix of whole grains and nuts and fruits really need toasting—and an added lace of oil and brown sugar?

Maximilian Bircher-Benner, MD, who created birkermuesli around 1900, didn't think so. Departing from the wisdom of the day, he concluded that diets of uncooked cereals, fruits, and vegetables—mere peasant food, his critics scoffed—would produce a vitality that rivaled the Swiss mountain air.

The good doctor's conviction cost him his membership in the medical society, but undaunted he founded a sanatorium in Zurich called Living Force. Under a regime of sunshine, exercise, fresh produce, and whole grains, many patients whose conditions had confounded traditional physicians were cured.

Pulled Strawberries

There's nothing like Oregon strawberries in June. Fragile berries similar to ours grow all around the country in backyards, u-pick patches, and on farms. They also show up at farmers' markets and in boxes left on doorsteps by family farmers who run consumer supported agriculture programs.

All you need for pulled strawberries are your hands and perfectly ripe berries. Pluck off the pert green caps, pull the berries apart, and let the Raggedy Ann edges and juicy red hearts speak for themselves.

On Strawberry Fields Forever?—

In addition to being so hard you have to smash them and so tasteless you have to add sugar, California berries produced by non-organic growers are grown in a questionable manner.

Picture huge tractors lumbering over the land dragging claws that inject the fumigant methyl bromide a foot down into the earth. Workers trudge behind with plastic sheeting that traps the chemical in the soil while it kills off all living organisms. In a few days when the sheets are lifted, the methyl bromide drifts off into

"There, lined up in small baskets, were strawberries smaller than the California berries Eden was used to, softer looking, their color darker and uniform, not with a green rim around the stems… in truth, their own little revelation, more fragile than any she had ever tasted. Eden said she'd take three boxes."

From *American Cookery: A Novel*, by Laura Kalpakian.

the air where it adds to the depletion of the ozone layer. And when new berries are planted, farmers have to add chemical fertilizers to the denuded soils.

Larry Eddings, owner of Pacific Gold, put a tenth of his 2005 strawberry production in organics. Although he thinks "methyl bromide is a whipping boy," he pointed out that the new model may well be the future for California growers.

"The truth in the berry business is that on the conventional side we're making very little money. It struck me eight years ago that there was a lot of talk in the organic world, so I've been turning some of my production that way," Eddings said. "It's turned out pretty well, and I like it a lot. We grow lovely berries, not gnarly little things with worm holes in them like I thought organics were before we got into this."

Apples with Beanpaste, Kasha, and Lime

I know legumes in the morning may sound weird, but this breakfast is way too delicious not to offer for your eating pleasure. Besides many of the world's people don't head off for creamy java and scones when they rise.

That's how it was when I lived in the Hopi mesa village of Sipaulovi in the 1980s. My neighbors, Joyce and Clark Tawayesva, with whom I frequently ate, were getting up in age and hadn't had a refrigerator for very many years. So Ma, as we called her, did like she always had and ate leftovers before they spoiled in the heat of the day. Our breakfasts were often warmed up hominy stew, blue cornmeal dumplings, or chile beans with homemade bread. At least hers and mine were. For his part, Pa didn't get into that groove anymore. He ate boxed cereal with his grand kids.

Recipe Note

Spread slices of your favorite eating apple with beanpaste. Sprinkle on kasha, cinnamon, and lime juice. Kasha, toasted F groats, is crunchy and wonderful right from the bulk bins. An ultrafast way to get your whole grains.

On a Roll with Fruit and Beanpaste—

In winter nothing's better than chunks of pear simmered in water with ginger and beanpaste. With a topping of cottage cream, kasha, and lemon juice this variation on the theme is fabulous.

Beanpaste

Recipe Note

Smash cooked beans with balsamic vinegar and pinches of salt, turmeric, and red chile flakes. A blender is the fastest way to get a creamy, fluffy paste. Pinto beans make for a peachy brown blend, while limas and white beans yield a lighter colored paste. Turn your sights on garbanzos, of course, and you're on your way to making hummus.

Thanksgiving Breakfast

There was a reason they didn't name me Patience, but I suspect I'm not the only one who finds food often tastes better when it's enjoyed ahead of the fact and out of the limelight.

Recipe Note

Onto half a baked sweet potato spoon KBJ's Cranberries (p. 36). Top with unsweetened whipped cream and nutmeg.

Details

I've always liked baked potato skins, so it wasn't a stretch to consider the jackets on sweet potatoes as edible. Especially when oiled prior to baking, sweet potato skins are soft and contrast wonderfully with the smooth orange flesh.

If you get a late start, run a metal skewer through the length of a tuber to shorten the baking time.

On a Roll with Whipped Cream—

I found that straight whipped cream didn't keep me as satisfied through the morning as I would have liked. So the next day when I repeated this charming breakfast, I folded what was left of the whipped into some cottage cream. It tasted just as sinfully delicious and was a better deal in terms of keeping the wolves at bay.

On Sweet Potatoes or Yams—

"There are two kinds of sweet potatoes in markets," Russ Parsons writes in *How to Pick a Peach* (2007). "One is pale orange and starchy; the other is dark orange, a little sweeter and very moist. Sweet potatoes are frequently called yams, although they are completely different from true yams, which hail from West Africa."

KBJ's Cranberries

My mother, Kathleen Brown Johnson, used her initials frequently, both when she worked in Washington DC for Senator Wayne Morse during the Second World War and later in life when raising her family. Thus the name for this holiday relish. Every year at Thanksgiving out would come the old-fashioned grinder—the hand crank affair that you secure to the counter top. It was how they made hamburger way back when, but KBJ used it to grind the fruit for her fresh relish. A bag of cranberries. A whole orange, peel and all. A cored apple. After Mom grew too fragile for the kitchen, I'd be instructed to make the relish each year. I still do—after a fashion.

Recipe Note

Smash some cranberries in a mortar with some orange segments. When you have a chunky pulp, fold in pomegranate seeds and a splash of the best brandy you can find.

On a Roll with Cranberries—

Not wanting to bother with the mortar and pestle the next morning when I wanted more relish, I simply stirred up a compote of whole cranberries, small Clementine orange segments, diced apple, and pomegranate seeds.

It was especially interesting to get acquainted with the taste and texture of whole cranberries. They were much better than I'd expected, their subtle, sour tones complementing the sweet fruits quite nicely.

Rolled Up Pancakes

They're called crepes today, but when I was growing up we just called them rolled ups. Mom made them on weekends because although they are easy, they do take time. If you give these a try and get some confidence going, know that they're great for corraling cooked vegetables as well.

Recipe Note

Beat in one egg for every cup of milk you use. Sprinkle in a little whole wheat pastry flour at a time and whisk. The goal is a silky batter comparable to a thin gravy. Add a pinch of salt and some vanilla, and let it set ten minutes or so.

Bring your pan up to medium heat and oil with a dab of butter. Then get ready to be quick on the draw. Ladle on some batter, very quickly lift the griddle, and swirl the batter around to coat the surface. Cook until the edges start to lift. Flip the thin pancake so the other side gets golden brown as well.

Details

Mom, and Aunt Kirsten Wilson who was also known for her rolled ups, used white flour for theirs. But once I got swept up in the late-1960s and its *Appetite for Change*—a phrase coined by Warren Belasco as the title for his book on "how the counterculture took on the food industry"—I've favored whole wheat pastry flour. Buckwheat flour also works as the world of blini makers well know. Actually, finely ground flours from the range of whole grains will work in rolled ups: cornmeal masa, quinoa, brown rice, millet, you name it.

The secret to rolled ups is being quick once the batter hits the griddle. It takes some practice, so expect rolled ups that look more like maps than perfect discs at first. Even these, though, will work since the edges are hidden once you roll them.

It's often the case that you have to go back and add more milk or flour to get a batter that flows just right. With patience, though, you'll find that making this special breakfast is not hard—only so time consuming that if you're cooking for a crowd you'll inevitably want to get two griddles going.

When I was young we ate rolled ups with butter and sugar, but these days a filling of warmed poached fruit and cottage cream sends me over the top. Sometimes I'll even go for pear wedges and beanpaste (p. 33). Then again, there's the Scandinavian way that Aunt Kirsten favored: butter and raspberry jam—or the more traditional lingonberry.

On Learning Curves—

If rolled-ups sound daunting to you, all you have to remember is to make them the next time grandpa's around. Then just whisper to him that no matter how they turn out, he's supposed to ooh and ahh. That's what they do in Hopiland. Cooks learning to make piki bread, something much more difficult than rolled-ups, always present their first efforts to grandpa. That's the patriarch's cue to tell the fledging cook how delicious her creation is and eat the offering with great delight, even if it's thick and the ladies are teasing her about how it looks a map.

On the Griddle—

There's nothing like a cast iron griddle. Not only does it carry heat that cooks evenly and browns beautifully, all there is to cleaning is a quick wipe with a cloth. Between my griddle and cast iron wok, each of which have staked out rather permanent claims on the stove top, there is little washing of pots and pans going on in my kitchen.

Bob's Polenta Waffles

Whoever thought waffles could be made from straight polenta without eggs or anything. These gorgeous golden waffles are crunchy and chewy and homey and good. Thanks to Bob Goforth's inventiveness on this one. It's a great big wow of a winner in my kitchen.

Recipe Note

Spoon freshly made polenta into an oiled waffle iron and bake. Enjoy with fresh fruit or check your pantry for a jar of home canned peaches. Or treat the waffle like toast and have it with scrambled tofu—or for lunch with soups and salads.

Details

I use one part polenta to two parts salted water. My polenta usually turns out pretty thick but I'm firm with the waffle iron lid in order to work the pretty yellow porridge out to the circumference. The waffles bake beautifully and release easily from the oiled surface.

On Cooking Polenta—

Bob and his wife Beth cook like I do and break all the rules. In other words we're busy working people and don't have time to stir polenta the requisite thirty to forty minutes on which so many insist. To make his waffles Bob said he stirred the polenta five to ten minutes. That's about what I do as well.

I suppose one reason I'm cavalier on polenta is because I lived ten years on the Navajo and Hopi reservations. By day I was a public school teacher, but by night I was in the kitchens of the local women where I stirred up my share of cornmeal.

So I think of polenta as simply the coarse ground meal it is, a grade that can take longer to cook than a fine grind if you want super creamy results, but one that works with shorter times as well.

On Polenta and Cornmeal—

Unfortunately most cornmeals and polentas, organic or not, are made from degerminated corn kernels. This means the hull and germ of the corn kernel are removed before grinding and what results is pure starch, a refined product comparable to white flour.

There is a source for unrefined ground cornmeals, though. Bob's Red Mill makes two packaged whole grain corn products, one called cornflour and the other labeled coarse cornmeal polenta.

Corncakes with Pepper Jack

These puppies get more than passing notice. They go with spicy breakfasts and function as fresh bread come lunch or dinner time. They also work baked up as small fry for starters. Like neighbor, Patrick Earnest, said, "We really enjoyed the other night with everyone. The little pancakes had to be my favorite ..... Yum!"

Recipe Note

To a couple beaten eggs add a half cup vinegared milk and a spoonful of oil along with a pinch of salt and soda. Stir in enough cornmeal to get a spoonable batter. Bake your corncakes on a medium griddle and sprinkle on grated pepper jack once you flip them. Use a lid to melt the cheese while the cakes finish cooking.

Details

You want to keep your heat no higher than medium with hotcakes so they won't burn while the first side is cooking. Watch for the bubbles that form in the surface. When there are lots of them, it's time for a flip.

On Vinegared Milk, Buttermilk, Yogurt, and Beer—

You can buy buttermilk which is already sour and certainly genteel. But vinegar's always on hand in my kitchen and making my own soured milk is cheaper. All it takes is a spoonful of vinegar to clabber a cup of milk—or if the truth be known I add the vinegar to the egg, milk, and oil, letting it do its thing right in the bowl.

There's also yogurt which in addition to sour power has all those healthful organisms. Since it's thicker than milk you'll, need to add a little water as well if you go this route. Or you can skip milk products altogether and use beer like the Wild West's grizzled prospectors did, either flat from the night before or splurging with a fresh bottle.

On a Roll with Corncakes—

I often add spaghetti squash and minced cilantro to corncakes, skipping the cheese altogether as pictured on p. 45.

Another twist is departing from the cornmeal and using leftover quinoa. An egg beaten into a half cup of salted quinoa and a little vinegar and soda yields a great batter for spooning onto the griddle.

On Fats and Cooking Oils—

Medical science tells us oils like olive, canola, and corn that are liquid at room temperature are our best choice. These oils are relatively benign because as mono and poly unsaturated fats, they lower total cholesterol including the bad stuff, LDL. At the same time they increase HDL, the good cholesterol.

On the other hand, saturated fats like butter that are solid at room temperature raise artery-clogging LDL. Research has also branded transfats, or partially hydrogenated oils like margarine and shortening, as so horribly hard on our bodies that many mainstream food producers have been willing, under recent pressure, to just say no.

—An additional word to the wise on olive oils: considerable controversy exists over the quality of olive oils many manufacturers are billing as 100 percent extra virgin. Apparently only with olive oils where we can see, taste, and smell the difference, are we getting sufficient quality to warrant the expense. Indeed, after Americans jumped on olive oil as the magic bullet for health, ignoring that the foodstuff is simply part of a well-rounded Mediterranean diet, the food industry did what it does: looked for ways to increase profits and capitalize on the craze.

Egg and Cheese Tacos

There's a universal appeal about food in tidy bundles you can pick up and eat—especially when they are sunny yellow and crispy crunchy. Just wrap this taco in some waxed paper, and you're out the door.

Recipe Note

Do a one egg omelet with cheddar cheese and keep warm in a low oven. Heat both sides of a corn tortilla on your griddle. Once it's softened and puffing up here and there, slip it half way under the omelet with a few cilantro fronds. Fold the tortilla over into a yellow half moon and chow down.

Details

Whisking up an egg with a spoon of water or milk takes seconds while a buttered griddle is heating on medium. Grated cheese melts easiest, but you can slice off thin pieces if you've no mind to mess with the grater. A key here is letting your egg cook until mostly set before putting the cheese on. That way you can easily fold the egg over the cheese with a spatula. If things get too hot, pull the griddle off the burner so the eggs don't burn on the bottom. Using a lid at this stage can also help melt the cheese and finish cooking the eggs.

If you have time to sit down to the table and eat this taco, try some fresh spinach along side as well as perhaps a slice of avocado and some salsa.

On Eggs and Omelets, Fluffy, Rich and Otherwise—

Read any book on French cooking and you'll get the royal scoop on using a balloon whisk to whip the bejeebers out of eggs, rendering them fluffy not stuffy. Also, adding rich things like cream or cream cheese to the eggs is 100 percent guaranteed to make them absolutely delicious.

I have used any number of these techniques, but regular eggs are lovely too. Eggs that are just beaten with a fork because you're in a hurry or don't have a whisk. Eggs that are done with a little water and scant fat to save the calories. The point is, of course, that when you cook according to your own rhythms, you are free to experiment with whatever approach best suits.

Here a Chick, There a Chick—

Hens who get to peck around like on Old MacDonald's Farm might be a minority at this point in history, but as Bob Dylan sang in his rusty 1960s voice, "the times, they are a-changin." In response to pressure from the Humane Society of the United States, Ben and Jerry's has pledged to stop using eggs from hens who live out miserable lives in batteries of cages stacked ten high in cavernous barns.

Such ideas are not new for Ben and Jerry's. The company's United Kingdom plant that produces ice cream for Europe has used cagefree eggs for years now. That's because British consumers have a record dating back to 1876 of insisting farm animals be treated humanely even if they all aren't out on Old MacDonald's any more.

"This new ethic is conservative, not radical," maintains Professor Bernard Rollan, who is widely recognized for pioneering the field of animal ethnics and policy during the 1970s. "It is a return to the roughly fair contract those who have husbanded animals for virtually all of human history have had with animals. That of taking great pains to put one's animals into the best possible environment one could find to meet their physical and psychological natures."

Making Sense of Egg Labels—

1. The cheapest eggs come from hens who live crammed together in cages without enough room to flap their wings, a behavior they try to do instinctively after they lay an egg.

2. Cagefree eggs are laid by hens freed from their cages into cavernous barns that hold thousands of birds.

3. Organic eggs are, by US Department of Agriculture definition, from hens that are supposed to have access to the outside. Apparently, however, the actual access these female birds have is a function of USDA oversight and the ethics of the grower. Moreover, even with these hens, explains Paul Shapiro, senior director of the Humane Society of the United States Factory Farm Campaign, "beak cutting and forced molting through starvation is permitted."

Increasing numbers of small farmers who treat hens humanely sell fresh, sustainably produced eggs at farmers' markets. For the most part these eggs don't carry organic designations because smaller growers have personal relationships with their clientele and can attest that their happy hens get to run and cluck and hunt and peck.

Cheesy Corn Bake

This puffy corn pudding is perfect for harvest when corn, zucchinis, and Anaheim chiles are spilling out of baskets everywhere.

Recipe Note

Grate the zucchini and cut the corn from the cob. Fold the vegetables into some eggs whisked with milk, cornmeal masa, turmeric, salt, and chile powder. Bake in a medium oven in an oiled dish until set. Garnish with sharp cheddar and serve with roasted Anaheims.

Details

The idea on the eggs is the same as for scrambled, so use just a spoon of milk or water to help them blend when you beat them with a whisk or fork. Then incorporate a little masa at a time until you have something close to a medium gravy.

Leave the cheese off until the end to keep it from burning. The bake will be hot enough when you pull it from the oven to melt a scattering of grated cheese.

On Roasting Green Chile–

As Hopi cooks know, roasted green chile makes all the differ- ence in a meal. It's easy to roast meaty Anaheims in a medium oven, either simply angled across the oven racks or on baking sheet.

Once they puff and blister, turn them until the second side is similarly done.

The rest is a community project, so stack the chiles on platter and join the party at the table. Green chile this way is *kwangwa*, Hopi for delicious.

You can also do like the Mexicans and wrap roasted chiles in a big tea towel to steam. Then the skins slip off easily, and you'll be left with whole tender flesh for rellenos or diced chile that cozies up to squash, quinoa, potatoes, beans, or eggs like it knew them well in former lives.

Starters & Sides

Having a little something to open a meal is such a nice gesture. As Laura Shapiro put it in her biography, *Julia Child*, our beloved French Chef encouraged American women to offer "a welcoming little first course." Even when I'm dining solo, I often sit down while things are cooking and eat some halved radishes spread with little bits of butter the way the French do. A crunchy, creamy treat indeed. For another ultrafast starter idea, see Beets and Chives.

If you have a bit more time and energy, the stovetop ideas range from the hands down most luscious recipe in this book, Edouard's Mother's Tomatoes, to the truly novel idea from the American Southwest, Fried Red Chile, Hopi-Style.

The Shrimp Cups are also definite taste treats for when you have a little more time and want to present your very best. And even though the pesto ideas are paired with particular recipes, either the classic Clifford's Mary Pesto or my own serendipitous creation Cashew Cilantro Pesto, easily lend themselves to dipping or dolloping hither and yon as the case presents.

Then, of course, there's roasting. Something wonderful happens to vegetables when they are shined up with a little oil and allowed to grown tender, sweet, and ultimately crispy in the oven. While the prep is ultrafast here, roasted vegetables do take some oven time. Whether you squeeze in a roast weeknights or reserve the pleasure for weekends, leftover morsels will make exceedingly welcome additions when savored midday at room temperature.

Starters & Sides

Oven-Roasted Nibbles
    Snap Beans with Pesto   60
    Clifford's Marvy Pesto   63
    Spiced Turnips and Cardamom Almonds   67
    Roasted Parsnips and Carrots   69
    Roasted Asparagus and Garlic Shoots   71
    Delicata Squash with Cashew Cilantro Pesto   74
    Cashew Cilantro Pesto   75
    Roasted Garlic   76
    Caramelized Onions, Oven-Style   78
Delectable Morsels from the Stovetop
    Fried Red Chile, Hopi-Style   81
    Beets with Chives   82
    Shrimp Cups   84
    Edouard's Mother's Tomatoes   85

Snap Beans with Pesto

In summer when snap beans are young and tender, a flash in the pan brings them to the table. But when harvest is on the wane and you feel like turning on the oven again, nothing's better than roasted beans. This version with pesto is easy and sensational enough to lure in the no-veg crowd. Serve these treats as starters or with a meal. Either way, if you leave them in the oven long enough to get crispy, they'll be grand.

Recipe Note

Toss the beans with pesto and roast in a medium oven on baking sheets or a cast iron griddle. Give them a stir after ten minutes. When done toss with more pesto.

Details

There's no need to buy jarred pesto. It's easy to make your own from the ideas in Clifford's Marvy Pesto (p. 63).

Take care to not crowd the beans. You want plenty of room so they roast, not steam.

To Stem Snap Beans or Not—

Without large aunts in print dresses around to help, stemming snap (or string) beans can be a lengthy, lonesome chore. Left with their stem ends on, beans turn into great finger food. Most people are game for this approach. Also if you're like me, you'll tend to make fresh snap beans more often when you don't have to stem them. The tender end tips of the beans are, of course, fine eating and never need trimming—something I learned from longtime family friend, Carole Branom, who discovered the approach by dining out in her share of five-star restaurants and cooking more than a few dishes of green beans herself.

On a Roll with Roasted Snap Beans—

Wintertime Roasts–Although green beans are clearly out of season in the winter, if you've put some by in your freezer they will roast nicely enough. Yellow and green beans, either whole or cut into smaller lengths, make a pretty mix with a cube or two of thawed pesto. Come those frigid days of January, a roast of pestoed beans puts a snap in your step.

Roasted Snap Beans with Olive Oil and Cumin– A puddle of oil in your hand—or a precise amount measured out if you're on a food plan that brooks no excess when it comes to fats. Work it over the beans with coarse salt, black pepper, and freshly ground cumin. You can even toast the cumin seeds in a dry skillet before grinding them. If you do, you won't be the only one to taste the difference. "These are nice," said neighbor Ryan Wayman who is discovering that he really likes fresh vegetables. "What's the spice?"

On Grinding Your Own Spices—

We share responsibly for the proliferation of pre-ground products, having demonstrated with our collective purchasing power that we will sacrifice quality for quick-fix convenience. But that's getting to be history as we increasingly wake up to how good food is when it's truly fresh—spices included.

The pleasure doesn't have to be reserved for professionals or the few home cooks who have half an afternoon to spend in their kitchens. When busy people don't have to fuss over a recipe by measuring and shopping for specific ingredients, we get in the mood for doing interesting things like grinding cumin seeds. The time factor is all of twenty seconds—or a minute if you include pouring the deeply enigmatic stuff of the Far East into a small jar for storing.

As vacuum pack java lured several generations down a detour away from coffee brewed with a fresh grind of beans, so too have the ground spice purveyors taken our palates on a flavorless romp.

Clifford's Marvy Pesto

Pesto is like mole, the famous Mexican sauce: it differs across a considerable range depending on region, families, and cooks. Those working in the nouvelle cuisine tradition have experimented with a variety of fresh herbs to create all kinds of new pestos. That said, there's nothing like the classic version made from sweet basil.

Recipe Note ·

Use either a mortar and pestle or food processor to turn fresh basil leaves, olive oil, garlic, walnuts, and Parmesan into a paste that's simply marvy, as my late brother Clifford Johnson would say.

Details

Some traditional pestos will be heavy on the garlic. Others will be quite nutty, with bold overtones of salty Parmesan. Clearly there's plenty of room for playing with ratios. That's a good thing, since the bunches of basil you'll have as a point of departure will differ every time.

I trolled several cookbooks and came up with the following guidelines. Try between two-thirds to a cup and a half of oil for every four cups of packed basil leaves. On garlic, one to four cloves seems to be the consensus. Similarly, there's a wide disparity on the nuts and cheese. Anywhere from a tablespoon to a cup of walnuts, or the more expensive pine nuts, and three-quarters to a cup and a half of grated Parmesan seems to be what those in the know favor.

After I get a batch of pesto made, I pick up a "Go to Directly to Lunch" card. Pesto smeared on thick slices of beefsteak tomatoes warmed in the summer sunshine. Not bad for a working woman.

Then I pack some pesto into a jar for use over the next several days, filming the top with oil to keep it from turning dark. The rest I freeze in ice cube trays. Once the cubes are hardened, the pesto gets popped out and stored in plastic freezer bags. A cube of thawed pesto in the winter is like a dollop of sunshine and goes great on everything from sandwiches and whole grains to eggs and spaghetti squash Also a cube or two melted into soups or warm salads can turn ho-hum fare into a fine feast with plenty of jazz.

Postscript on Pesto—

During harvest when basil is prolific, I'll often dispense with the goodies and just whiz up the leaves with some olive oil for freezing. Then come winter when thawing the cubes, I add whatever I'm a mind to.

I thought things were pared down about as far as they could go, but Bob and Beth Goforth, friends who garden in Northern Arizona, upped the ante. They put their basil up with nothing more than water. It turns deeply, righteously evergreen, the color of the Colorado Plateau's ponderosa pine forests. Come winter when cedar burning in their wood stove keeps their kitchen cozy, there's the bare bones basil all ready and waiting.

Get Thyself a Smashing Device—

Great cooking doesn't take fancy equipment–or much equipment. There are, though, a few things that can really help the cause, and one is a nice deep mortar and pestle. As you can see, the mortar I use is clay and the pestle is nothing more than a stout piece of wood for pounding away.

I didn't have such a marvel until a visit to Bangkok, and the generous cook I met there, Daeng Arporn Punlert, made sure I toted one back in a duffle. Yet, once home, this new smashing device sat for months on top of the refrigerator untouched.

Even after I called Rula Awwad-Rafferty, Jordanian-American friend, for coaching on tabbouleh, and she spoke not in terms of mincing but of "pounding" the garlic with salt, I did not take the cool, clay mortar in my hands.

But eventually came a hot August evening when I thought it would be more pleasant to pound up a pesto than it would to endure the roar of the blender. Not entirely trusting the process, I did give the basil, garlic, and walnuts a rough chop before shunting them into the mortar. But after that, it was merely a pour of olive oil and some rather fabulous smashing to produce a lovely result.

A smashing device is just like plucking chickens used to be. You can get in there and go for it, and once you're done whatever stress you had when you started has flown the coop.

No wonder Mediterraneans have traditionally done proper pestos this way. It's fun, quick, and the result has character.

Plus, rinsing the mortar is a breeze, way better than dealing with food processor clean-up.

All it takes it a couple times using a hand tool like this to find out that it's actually easier than powering up. Between that and the superior results, and you'll most likely be a convert—especially when you're doing small batches.

Spiced Turnips and Cardamom Almonds

Starters are tricky since you don't want people to fill up before they get to the table. This one worked well with guests on Christmas Eve. The humble turnips and hardy rosemary were straight from the garden that day; the cardamom freshly ground.

Recipe Note

Rub turnip wedges with a nice oil like toasted sesame and dust with coarse salt and cayenne pepper. Roast in a medium oven, turning after ten minutes for even browning. Toast almonds in the oven, toss with melted butter, and dust with cardamom. Fill the serving plate with roasted turnips. Scatter almonds and a few pomegranate seeds over the top.

Details

Cut the turnips in half and then into wedges. Spend a minute refining the wedges into smaller triangular pieces that are fairly uniform. You'll basically end up with two batches, one for guests and another for eating the next day. If you're simply roasting the turnips as a side dish, rustic cuts are great.

Do take the trouble to shuck a pomegranate. These glistening ruby seeds dazzle and bring festive bursts of tart flavor that play against the dense winter roots and nutmeats.

Capsicum Quotient—

I was a young woman when I shook as much flaked red pepper on my pizza as I did Parmesan cheese. The pie was inedible. Completely.

In was the same when I lived on the Hopi mesas and accepted a pickled jalapeno from a can two brothers were relishing. I thought the blazing fire in my mouth would never subside.

So when I first summoned the interest and courage to try cayenne pepper later in life, I measured out an eighth of a teaspoon for a recipe like I was handling the power of the sun itself.

If I were to credit a cuisine for selling me on the goodness of hot chile peppers it would have to be Thai. Granted, I started using more cayenne in my food months before I visited Thailand. Yet, while in the balmy tropics I experienced the sensational way a touch of chile truly enlivens food.

In the winter when fresh green chiles aren't available, dried red chile reigns. Cayenne, for example, is simply dried, ground cayenne peppers. Then there are the generic red chile flakes, not to mention a wide variety of whole red chiles in cellophane packages in the Mexican food aisles of groceries. You can crush these chiles yourself or fry them up Hopi-style. (See p. 81.)

Roasted Parsnips and Carrots

French fry lovers will almost always give a plate of roasted parsnips and carrots a big nod of approval.

Recipe Note

Slice parsnips and carrots on the diagonal. Shine them up with some good oil. Rub with paprika, coarse salt, and cracked pepper. Roast on a tray in a medium oven turning the roots after fifteen minutes so each side gets golden brown.

Details

Parsnip peelings are tougher than carrot and, depending on how thick you slice your pieces, can be too much chew for some people. Experimenting, doing one root with the peel and another without, is one way to find out what you think. (Remembering that many nutrients lie just below the skin in vegetables and fruits might make you more predisposed to give the peelings a serious chance.)

Hot from the oven these roasted roots are superb with homemade ketchup. To make this red brew, thin tomato paste with orange juice and vinegar, and season with garlic, oregano, coriander, and orange zest.

On Coarse Salt—

I love this stuff which is why I use it almost across the board. A small dish sits out near my chopping block. It's hunky-chunky enough to make food sparkle, and it makes such a statement that it doesn't take much.

Leave it to the Spaniards to lend fiery romance to paprika by smoking it over oak. Indeed, smoked paprika is getting lots of ink in food magazines these days. That's because smoked food of any stripe—cheese, salmon, or paprika—tastes so very excellent.

On Paprika—What a lovely way Europeans preserve sweet red peppers: first drying them and then grinding them into fine red powder that does so much more than decorate deviled eggs.

Paprikas vary according to the peppers and processing. There's hot zippy paprika from sweet reds and good old mild like our grandmas used, both styles from Hungary. I got lucky, and friends John and Beverly Rupp brought home darling sacks of both kinds from a recent trip to Eastern Europe. However it reaches your kitchen, though, paprika's a honey with its come hither, red sass.

Roasted Asparagus and Garlic Shoots

Bunny Lowman's actions may have pointed the way, but the pleasure of adding roasting to my kitchen craft was all mine—and came in its own time. Also when I finally did get around to roasting one June day after the early asparagus spears had given way to more portly stalks, I discovered the charm that garlic shoots added to the mix.

Recipe Note

Rub spears of asparagus and garlic shoots with good oil, coarse salt, and cayenne pepper. Roast in the oven, stirring after ten minutes.

Garlic Shoots—

Farmers' markets and consumer supported agriculture farms generally offer garlic in the spring because the mild, tender shoots make for such great eating. Garlic shoots are delightful sautéed in butter and make a unique accompaniment for anything from steamed millet to wild salmon.

It was Bunny Lowman who roasted the first asparagus I ever tasted, each spear arranged politely on a party tray to tantalize. Little did she know she inspired a revolution in my kitchen, although it was a good two years between when I tasted Lowman's asparagus and I roasted so much as a carrot.

Sigh. Such resistance overcoming inertia.

On Roasting Vegetables—

Vegetables roast marvelously well from low to high temperatures. On highs around 450 F, colors are preserved but you have to watch things like a hawk. Medium ovens of 350 work well too, and depending on what you're roasting, munchies will be yours in a half hour. Then again, if you're going out for a walk, you can turn the oven to 250. When you return, you'll have the sweetest caramelized morsels a soul could ever ask for.

My preferred roasting vehicle is—or was—Jessie Branom's extra large cast iron skillet. The iron and the sides of the pan cradle the vegetables in a cocoon of heat that caramelizes, and they turn out sweet and golden. Baking trays work, too, but as you'll discover if you use both vehicles like I usually do, the results cast iron produces are decidedly superior. Yet, at this writing, a new over-sized cast iron skillet is on my shopping list. Here's why.

Jessie Branom and my mother were close friends in Phoenix during the early 1960s where they raised their families. Jessie had two children; Mom had four. So the women reasoned that my mother should have the big frying pan Jessie owned, and Jessie should have my mother's medium sized skillet. The swap was made, and much later after Mom passed away Jesse's skillet came to me. I used it for years, but as a historian who thinks in terms of centuries, I'm aware of how numbered our days are—and how things can get lost in the shuffle at the end of life. So it was that Thanksgiving of 2007 when Jessie's first granddaughter married, I posted the skillet swathed in wedding wrap. As I wrote to the young bride, Jenny Branom Patberg, "Great scratch cooks have used this skillet for a half century. May its journey go on."

Delicata Squash with Cashew Cilantro Pesto

Delicata is my newly discovered favorite winter squash along with its plump little sister, sweet dumpling. No need for brown sugar and butter with these babies. Plus the jackets are usually soft enough to eat like baked potato skins. I must thank the Rose City Park Presbyterian Church for the find. The congregation practically gives away produce it gleans from the Hollywood Farmers' Market all during the growing season.

Recipe Note

Halve the squashes and invert on a rimmed tray to bake a half hour. When soft and cooled some, scoop out the seeds, slather on cashew cilantro pesto, a chop of fresh tomatoes, lime juice, and cayenne.

Details

You can easily cut this taste treat into slices for a starter.

In quarters or full halves, it makes a knock out side dish.

If tomatoes are out of season when you try delicata, stuff the cavity with a whole grain like quinoa that you've doctored with caramelized onions and winter savory. Or you might try some tofu spiked with red chile flakes.

Cashew Cilantro Pesto

You'd never think of missing the cheese in this pesto.

Recipe Note

Put cilantro leaves including the smaller stems in a blender with good olive oil, cashews, garlic, salt, and enough water to get a green goddessy sauce going. Presto. You have pesto.

It's All in What You Have on Hand—

This creamy pesto sprang to life one day when a couple bunches of cilantro from the church's gleaning table needed using and the only nuts in the house were cashews. Such predicaments life brings…

Roasted Garlic

You can roast garlic cloves like you do any vegetable, right in its own skin. These ivory crescents work as a delicious starters alongside Greek olives.

Recipe Note

Break up a bulb of garlic and oil the individual cloves with their jackets on. Roast on a tray in a medium oven.

Details

A clove of garlic is pretty small, so it doesn't take long in the oven. Give the loose cloves a stir after five minutes. Another option is doing them in a covered casserole, but I find what I usually end up doing is simply scattering some in when I roast other vegetables like carrots, peppers, turnips, parsnips, and rutabagas.

Celebrating a Moment with Fresh Garlic—

Feeling the knobby garlic in the palm of your hand. The weight of it. Solid and true.

The crackling sound that comes when you pull away the papery covering from a bulb. The translucence of the parchment paper when you hold one thin slip to the light.

Postscript on Roasted Garlic—

For years I thought the only way to roast garlic was slice the end off a whole bulb and bake it in a foil tent. When it was done I'd squeeze the garlic out of its husk and have some fabulous paste to spread on whole wheat brushchetta. Roasted garlic is so very splendid done that way, but it's sort of a pain and you lose so much in the process. Besides, I find I roast garlic more often when it's not quite so complicated.

Caramelized Onions, Oven-Style

Sliced onions caramelize magnificently in a slow oven, filling the air with an aroma to write home about. More, there's no standing at the stove and stirring.

Recipe Note

Brown the onions stove top in a little oil under a lid to get their juices flowing. Then put them uncovered into a slow, slow oven with enough water added now and then to keep the onions moist. As always, cast iron holds the heat and yields stellar results.

Details

To slice onions easily, cut in half and put the flat side down on your board. When you reach that awkward point, turn the onion to a new plane and continue slicing, repeating the process until you're down to the nubbins. If you must have all the pieces the same length, just give your longer ones a quick chop.

Two onions are about all I can do at once without tears coming. That's enough, though, since they yield a nice full jar once they're cooked down.

Like caramelized onions done on the stove top, sliced onions slow roasted in the oven turn into a limp, jammy brew that can serve as a sumptuous relish. Think grilled cheese sandwiches or pita bread with hummus. These sublime onions also add dimension to most any soup or composed salad you are conjuring up. They make whole grains and legumes perk right up as well—and as the meat-eaters on our street can attest, they go great with things like Texas brisket and celebratory champagne. Truly, there's not much not to like about a batch of sliced onions slow roasted in your oven.

Fried Red Chile, Hopi-Style

With a skillet of fried chile in the center of the table, people can dip in as they eat, spearing a bit of chile and swirling whatever else is on their fork in the warm oil. If you're at a Hopi table expect things like pork chops, hard boiled eggs, and little corn dumplings called blue marbles. If you're at an Anglo table you might find yourself dipping salmon or even—as Susan Isaacs sensibly did— simply spooning up some of the chile and oil to season the rice on your plate.

That said, know that if you do try dipping into the common pot, Hopi manners require that each person stay in their own corner of the pan. It's rather like the Columbia tribes' salmon fishing philosophy: "I fish on this side. You fish on that side. Nobody fish in the middle."

Recipe Note

Use long dried red chile like guajillos or Anaheims. First break off the hot core ends and shake out most of the equally hot seeds. Then break the chiles into four or five nice pieces and fry them in a half inch of medium hot oil, turning them for even browning.

Use a small, heavy-bottomed skillet that will go to the table nicely. Trying a test piece in the pan is a smart move because you want the oil hot enough to crisp and darken the chile without burning it, something that can easily happen if you're not paying attention.

Beets with Chives

One of the dishes served at Elizabeth David's memorial gathering in 1992 was "baby beetroots and chives." I usually can't get baby beets, but I love this simple dish all the same. The sweet beets sparked with little snips of oniony chive are refreshing as spring begins to take over from winter.

Recipe Note

Boil up a pot of beets. Cool, trim, and slip the skins off. Slice into pretty chunks or discs. Splash with cider vinegar. Garnish with plenty of finely snipped chives using your kitchen scissors.

On Fats in Our Diets—

There's no fat in Beets and Chives which ought to please people like myself who notice that when they start getting frisky with oils, butters and whatnot, unwanted pounds settle in.

It's true that bowing down to the lowfat alter has passed us by and current wisdom from nutritionists is that we need respectable amounts of fat in our diets. Defining what respectable amounts means, though, is the ticket.

But that's the beauty of measure free approaches to cooking. If your health will take a little more fat, drizzle it on. If not, go for the vinegar as I did in this light, lovely spring dish.

Shrimp Cups

This dish came about rather serendipitously. There was this nifty cast iron pan with little indentations at the Asian market that I couldn't resist. Then there were memories of egg foo young from my childhood plus some leftover prawns and vegetables. How nice and tidy they were contained in their little roundness. (Photo p. 57.)

Recipe Note

Stir an egg or two into leftover vegetables (for these I had a mix of spaghetti squash, chopped kale, and red and green peppers) and cook either in a buttered cast iron pan with indentations like the one I found at the Asian market or simply bake by the big spoonful (like mini egg foo young) on a griddle. Decorate with cooked prawns sliced in half widthwise. Serve with Dijon mustard.

Details

If you're using a pan with round indentations, use a pastry brush to sweep the melted butter up around the sides. Fill the holes almost to brimming, allowing room for the cups to puff some.

A lid and medium heat helps the eggs cook and keeps the bottoms from burning. Use a soup spoon to easily remove the shrimp cups from the pan.

Edouard's Mother's Tomatoes

Renowned British food writer, Elizabeth David, respected Dr. Edouard de Pomiane because the scientist brought experiment, discipline, and humility to his culinary pursuits. "Out of all of it," David writes, "he appears to have extracted, and given, an uncommon amount of pleasure." Clearly that's the case with this "hot first dish" that he attributed to his Polish mother. As David writes, "his method makes tomatoes taste so startlingly unlike any other dish of cook tomatoes." To that I'd add, Edouard's Mother's Tomatoes are the yummiest recipe in this book.

Recipe Note

Slice tomatoes in half and cook them in butter on both sides, piercing the skins so the juices run out. Turn them back and forth until you have some red gems that are calling to you. Then pour some good cream over the works and heat through.

Details

As usual, you can mix and match and still make it to the dance. The first few times I tried these tomatoes, all I had was mascarpone, Italian cream cheese that I buy everything once in a while because it's irresistible.

The mascarpone worked great, as did some sour cream on another go-round.

Then there was the lower fat option of buttermilk that I tried. Not nearly as splendid, but an option if the unctuous creamy potions aren't in a person's repertoire.

Talk about some heavenly yum that tastes like the goddesses made it. Edouard's mother might have been Polish, but she wasn't joking around when she concocted this luscious dish.

Soups

Soups and moods. They seem to go together since a person either gets in the mood for a special bowl of soup, or a certain soup puts a person in a particular mood. Yes, soups are evocative. They bring back memories and create new ones. Served piping hot or icy cold, soups complement the weather, they nourish, they please.

There's so much more to soups than recipes, though. That's why even though there are just five soups offered in this chapter, you'll find enough ideas to enlarge your repertoire gracefully and easily.

That's because soups are immensely forgiving. They can accommodate perfectly fresh ingredients, pave the way for using leftovers, start with very particular stocks, or simply develop flavor on their own merits right in the pot.

Soups can contain identifiable chunks of vegetables or wind up as lean and lovely creamy purees. Or dishes that don't quite turn out can become soups—just consult Julia Child's writings as she knew all about the idea of saving a ruined dish by gleefully letting it morph right along into the soup pot.

Any way it comes together, as generations of Americans have grown up knowing, soup really is good food.

Soups

Five Soups for Five Moods

Tropical
>Hot and Sour Shrimp Soup, Thai-Style   92

Winter
>Minestrone with Millet   96

Spring
>Soupy Soup with Cauliflower and Lima Beans   100

Summer
>Cucumber Melon Soup   105

Autumn
>Salmon Chowder
>with Roasted Tomatoes and Sweet Peppers   108

Hot and Sour Shrimp Soup, Thai-Style

Use home canned or frozen tomatoes if you have some put by.

And should you spy a bag of roasted bell peppers while the freezer's open, know that they rub shoulders with their tomato sisters in this soup like there's no tomorrow.

"Shrimp boats is a comin' there's dancin' tonight!" Funny how those lines you sang as a child sail back by. Especially when it's February and your heart yearns for something beyond the pale. The recipe note below is from notes I made while visiting friends Doug and Sandy Kypfer in Bangkok and watching their faithful cook and friend, Daeng Arporn Punlert, make tom yam goong.

Recipe Note

Boil the shells from your prawns in a pot of water and strain. Add garlic, lemon grass, woody ginger (galangal), red onion and keep the boil going. Then tomatoes and mushrooms, not backing off from the high heat. After ten minutes or so cut the heat and put your shrimp in with some lime leaf and pounded Thai chiles. Just before serving add a chop of fresh coriander and lime juice. And yes, you sort of pick your way through the pieces of lemon grass, woody ginger, and lime leaf as you eat. It's half the fun.

Details

There's an Asian grocery close to me, so I can find the exotics. But if you aren't inclined to search out those things, you'll still get a wonderful hot and sour broth from the chiles and lime juice.

If you don't have a mortar and pestle, minced chiles (or just one if you're a tenderfoot) will work. It's just that when you pound chiles down to a pulp, they blend ever so nicely into whatever you're making.

Turn the fire on high on under a heavy bottomed soup pot when you start slicing and dicing. That way when the vegetables hit the broth there's plenty of heat. Since only the onions need to soften, this fresh soup doesn't take more than fifteen minutes.

There's little way you can miss on the ratios. A half an onion is usually a good starting point along with a clove of garlic and about the same amount of minced ginger.

You'll notice there's no fat in this soup, but no need to feel deprived. Thais make many of their soups and salads without oil, relying on spices and sours for flavor.

Overcooked, tough shrimp is nobody's friend and served up more times than not—especially when people grill it. All prawns need is a flash in the heat after you've de-veined them by making a slit down the back and rinsing out the brown stringy thing. So whether you peel them ahead as in this soup or let people at the table get in on it, once prawns turn pink they're succulent and good to go.

Not interested in shrimp? Try legumes like black beans, pintos, garbanzos, or limas. No go on beans? There's always tofu or tempeh, tofu's fermented cousin.

Fresh cilantro's so worth the trouble. Even in miniscule amounts cilantro (like fresh parsley) ratchets the flavor bar up several impressive notches. Just take care to add it right before you eat so it keeps its brilliant emerald somewhere-over-the-rainbow hue.

On Fish Sauce—

Strange name, perhaps, but don't underestimate the power of fish sauce. It's made from flavor-packing anchovies and brings a salty interest to food that plain salt doesn't provide. If you like Thai food, you like fish sauce because there's hardly a dish the Thais make that doesn't rely on this heavenly brew.

Salt and Pepper v. Fish Sauce and Chile—

I often use fish sauce and red chile as a stand in for salt and pepper. My reasoning is that they have more character than regular old salt and black pepper. But take my approach with a grain of whatever. Clearly there's a reason the western world has enshrined salt and pepper to the degree that the happy couple have special shakers crafted for them.

Minestrone with Millet

This riff on Italy's classic soup breaks with tradition in more ways than passing on pasta. It shows how many of the rules we can bend—like skipping the onion sauté or the adding of the sacred bay leaf—and still come up with good food. Yes, when we've time, taking pains is great. But also yes, on evenings after work, busy people can take considerable creative license and find their efforts handsomely rewarded.

Recipe Note

Start with water, tomatoes, and salsa. Add sliced leeks, grated carrot, cooked pinto beans, and leftover millet. Stir in fish sauce, balsamic vinegar, black pepper, and red wine. Cut the heat and fold in a rustic chop of kale. Garnish with diced Parmesan.

Details

Because pintos are what I had, I used then instead of the white beans you typically find in minestrones. Visually white beans are prettier in this red broth, but pink pintos made their own unique statement and were worthy enough for the weekday table.

I like to taste before and after the fish sauce, wine, vinegar, chile

I used salsa here because fresh peppers were a distant memory the winter day I first made this minestrone. Also, I didn't feel like dealing with an onion and thought some salsa would bring complexity.

It did not disappoint. Rather this wonderful creation by our Latin American neighbors showed itself entirely up to the task of courting an Italian inspired soup.

stages so that I get practiced at appreciating what each of these highly significant elements does to food. When in doubt err on the conservative side. A big spoonful of fish sauce is a good beginning. A pinch of chile. A spritz of vinegar. A polite pour of wine, knowing that with this latter element a little time is needed for it to marry with the broth.

Vinegar turns greens darkly unappetizing in short order. If you're not going to serve pronto, you can put uncooked chops of kale in the bowls and simply ladle the steaming hot minestrone over when it's time to eat. The greens will wilt down in seconds with a stir or two. Whatever approach you take, the key is to not miss the fresh scent of the greens that so persuasively grounds a soul in the here and now.

On Leeks and Less Familiar Vegetables—

Instead of feeling bound to do something special with leeks because they are somewhat unusual, I allow myself to use them as needed in things like this soup. This means I don't have to go digging for the potato and leek recipe—and then go to the store for the missing ingredients. It also means that I'm more inclined to buy leeks and other less familiar vegetables than I might otherwise.

Millet's Not Just for the Birds—

The point about how our wild birds are better fed than we are because they eat whole grain millet has been made before. Yet, if you're still laboring under the mantle of white pasta like so many of us, here's a chance to take flight. Put cooked millet in your minestrone. It won't hurt, and it's easy to do up a pot of this light colored grain.

Use one part millet to two parts salted water, bringing things to a boil before turning to low and covering. The fluffy yellow grain will be done in twenty minutes and have such a heavenly head of steam that you might decide to repeat the experiment again some time.

Freshly steamed millet is great with any number of goodies like scallions, walnuts, or a chop of fresh apricots. Mostly, though, all it needs is a drizzle of good oil or a pat of creamery butter to take its place proudly at the table.

On Cooking with Wine—

A fermented foodstuff, wine brings umami to foods. Umami is that unidentifiable mouth feel people find so enticing.

I've made carrot soup, for example, both with and without white wine. You have to let the wine cook into the soup a bit, of course, but once it does, there's really no comparison on which version has more depth of flavor and interest.

Yet, if wine isn't something you choose to use, leave it out. You can develop umami in other ways like using fish sauce.

Soupy Soup with Cauliflower and Limas

The sunny April day I first made this soup, I stepped outside to pet Soupy, the elderly doggie who used to live next door with her mommy, Marsha, and her sister, Ruby. What could I do but name the soup after her.

Recipe Note

Add a chop of savoy cabbage, onion, and cauliflower to nothing more than a boil of water and pinch of turmeric for color. Finish this cleanly flavored soup with cooked lima beans, a drizzle of good oil, the zest and juice from a lemon, and a chop of flat leaf parsley.

Details

A cruet of good oil on the table is nice, and one that those watching their fat intake will appreciate since they can control their serving size.

If you can find it, savoy cabbage with its wrinkly-crinkly leaves is, as the kids used to say, "boo-ful." If not regular cabbage is a stalwart stand-in.

On Soup Stock—

The point at which cookbooks start talking about making stock is often the place where I make a mental shift from thinking I might try the recipe to that of simply reading about it. I have made lovely vegetable stocks like court bullion in my time. But these days fussing like that is out of the question; I'm too busy. So I build my broths right in the pan like Thais do. Sometimes, as with this soup, I don't even bother with spices and let the vegetables shine on their own.

None other than the French country cook, Lulu Peynaud, did too. As she told food writer Richard Olney, "I prefer soups prepared with water—with stock, you can't taste the vegetables."

And then there's the *grande dame* herself, Julia Child weighing in with her magnum opus, *The Way to Cook*. There she writes that the ubiquitous chicken stock we tend to use so automatically masks the more delicate vegetable flavors.

On Cruising with Some Zip—

I first encountered using mustard seeds in cooking in one of my favorite cookbooks, *Laurel's Kitchen*. It was an East Indian dish and their recipe called for putting black mustard seeds into hot oil in a heavy bottomed pan, keeping the lid firmly in place until the furious popping quieted.

I still use this method occasionally since it's so uncommonly fun. But mostly I put the mustard seeds directly into the broth. They are still plenty jazzy, and whether you use brown or yellow, expect a tiny mustardy rush when you bite down on one. However they're prepared, I'll put my faith in mustard seeds any day.

On Turmeric—

This queenly spice is an essential element in most soups, warm salads, and egg dishes. That's because golden turmeric warms the color of whatever you're making. Just be sure to use it sparingly, as too much turmeric can bring an unwanted flavor to food.

Breathe Deep the Gathering Aromatics—

The aromatics—onions, garlic, ginger—have volatile elements that are released when they are sautéed in oil. This treatment sharpens the flavors and hence is the standard approach most recipes in the western tradition take. In the spirit of both cutting back on oil and in the Thai-style of using no oil at all in many dishes, I frequently opt for omitting the sauté and instead simply treat the aromatics as I do the rest of the vegetables by putting them into the broth to soften. In the process they take on a mild flavor and bits of garlic that get through larger than they might are sweet and not offensive.

Cucumber-Melon Soup

Recipe Note

Give chilled cucumbers and cantaloupe a spin in the blender with a seeded jalapeno, salt, pepper, and tarragon vinegar. Garnish this lean and serene drinkable smoothie with slivers of melon or toasted coconut.

Details

The ends of most cucumbers are bitter, so it's nice to trim them away. The peeling, though, isn't offensive to me—at least when I'm using round, yellow lemon cucumbers. Even if I have the more common green cukes, sometimes I'll won't take off the peeling, since my grandmother never did when she made her sweet and sour cucumbers.

She simply scored the peelings vertically with a fork to make a pretty edge before she sliced them thinly and put them down to marinate in a dressing of white vinegar, sugar, salt, and pepper. Ah yes, how I loved Grandma's cucumbers.

One jalapeno packs plenty of spicy kick, so use sparingly and remove the membranes and seeds where more heat than most want resides. Keep your hands away from your face and wash them well after working with hot peppers. Seriously.

Tarragon vinegar conveys a mystique, but sometimes I wonder if my palate could pass a taste test. Whatever the case, I imagine most any white vinegar would work here.

On a Roll with Cucumber Soup—

Sweet melons inevitably get eaten long before the cucumber supply abates. That's when I put tomatoes and onions in the blender with the cucumbers and perhaps some leftover brown rice. With some red wine vinegar, fish sauce, pepper, and a handful of soynuts for garnish, lunch is served once again.

I suppose you could call this version a gazpacho. All I know is that I had my soup done and was enjoying it in the time it would have taken to wade through the elaborate, complicated gazpacho recipes I read while I was eating.

Cucumber-Melon Soup is perfect
for those scorching hot days
at summer's end.
And wouldn't you know
that's precisely
when cucumbers and melons
are in
their prime.

Salmon Chowder with Roasted Tomatoes and Sweet Peppers

I'm half Norwegian and we Norskes love our cold salmon and dilled cucumbers. Still, when fall starts to bluster, there's nothing like chowder. Between the leftover roasted salmon and vegetables, this solo lunch took five minutes to make.

Recipe Note

Put leftover roasted tomatoes and peppers in a pot on medium heat. Add leftover quinoa, cold salmon, and milk. Season with lemon juice, salt, and pepper. Garnish with minced parsley and butter.

Details

Something fresh and green, dill or parsley, makes the soup inviting. Keep in mind that dried herbs aren't really too cool. Some things like tomatoes and grapes dry to excellent advantage, but more often dehydrated food like carrots, onions, potatoes, and herbs lose the appeal they had when fresh. Still, the first time I made this soup I just used dried dill weed. It might have done little for the flavor, but visually it made a pretty statement and it did have a faint lingering hint of the summer crop. Or maybe it was the pat of butter in my bowl that turned me into a purring cat as I tasted the first excellent spoonfuls of this quick midday repast for one.

On Fresh Herbs—

Clearly I'm not the best when it comes to using fresh herbs, but my friend Laura Berg has it down. "What a great idea," I said when I noticed the herb bouquet she keeps in a vase of water on her kitchen window sill.

"Yes," she said, fingering dainty sprigs of thyme, and the bolder stems of rosemary, sage, and both kinds of parsley she gathered from patches dotting her garden. "I love it too. It's so handy when I'm in the middle of cooking."

On Chowders for the Gang—

Once you have your first bowl of chowder after the weather gets cold, you usually will want more in a few days. On this go-round I was more traditional and started diced onion and minced garlic in a big pot with some oil. In went diced potatoes along with enough water to get things going over medium heat. Then came chopped tomatoes, peppers, and a pour of white wine.

I was out of roasted tomatoes so used fresh ones lingering from harvest, but there were still some soft smoky peppers ready to give their sweet flesh over to the greater good.

After that, in went the salmon, although to beef up the protein I added cooked white beans from a pot in the fridge. Technically, the legumes morphed the chowder over into the land of minestrone. But for me it was still chowder because at that point although I added several more tomatoes to embolden the red broth, I decided that I couldn't live without milk and poured in the creamy white stuff to turn the soup a darling, pale coral.

For seasoning, I turned to magical fish sauce. I also still had some fresh hot peppers from the garden, so minced one of these along with some fresh fennel fronds that worked to remarkably good advantage.

That was it. I had a delectable pot of chowder. It was ready to serve a crowd or go into the fridge to be savored all through the week. I could have some frozen in small cartons as well—if we hadn't dispatched it so eagerly.

On the Artistry of Cooking—

"I often feel guilty when writing recipes. To capture what one can of elusive, changing experience—a fabric of habit, intuition, and inspiration of the moment—and imprison it in a chilly formula composed of cups, tablespoons, inches, and oven temperatures," writes Richard Olney, "is like robbing a bird of flight.

On Lemon Juice and Sours—

It's common knowledge in professional cooking circles that lemons, limes, or vinegars brighten the flavor of food famously, even as they remain indiscernibly in the background. Chef Doug Flicker even squeezes a sagacious few drops of lemon juice into his mashed spuds, so declared Holly Hughes in her *Best Food Writing* anthology from 2005.

So, no need to reserve lemons for fish. There's little that doesn't benefit from a squeeze of sour citrus or a few drops of tangy vinegar.

Salads

Salads. Warm. Cool. Composed. Otherwise. These days salads are more than skimpy little bowls of lettuce with bottled dressing. Indeed, they easily take center stage and become the meal.

Still, old ways cling and generally when people say salad, they mean a dish containing mostly low calorie vegetables like lettuce, cucumbers, tomatoes, onions, cabbage, and radishes with perhaps a weighty carrot or two grated in "for color."

This chapter offers some light weight salads in that tradition, but mostly its focus is on riotous composed salads that stick to your ribs. The beauty of eating this way is that you can dabble in the full palette of seasonal vegetables Mother Nature provides. Paired with all manner of fruits, nuts, legumes, cheeses, and grains, and dressed to kill in good oils and lovely sours, vegetable salads are indeed good eating.

As neighbor and financial planner in his twenties, Ryan Wayman, said, "I'd never eat all this healthy stuff on my own. But it is true, Jean. You have opened my eyes to a whole new world of food. I just love it!"

I can't remember exactly which salad won Wayman's heart, but it might have been the Spicy Cilantro Salad. After all, when you add white chocolate chips, pineapple, and cashews to food, it usually sells pretty well in River City. Then again it might have been the dear Greens with Pears and Swiss. Clearly more delicate but perfect with prawns flash cooked in butter and some steamed brown rice. Or perhaps it was the Sweet Basil with Tomatoes and Mozzarella that works so great for gardeners who don't want to make pesto out of all their surplus. Who knows. The main thing is that Wayman is interested. He's allowing for the possibility that fresh vegetables really can taste great when they're prepared with a little savvy.

Salads

Salad for Four Seasons

Winter
      Red and Yellow Beets with Blue Cheese   116
      Greens with Pears and Swiss   120
Spring
      Spring Salad on a Theme of Radishes and Jicama   127
      Quinoa with Peapods and Avocado   131
Summer
      Spicy Cilantro Salad
        with White Chocolate, Pineapple, and Cashews   134
      Sweet Basil with Tomato and Mozzarella   138
Fall
      Thai Slaw   139
      Carrot Slaw with Frozen Grapes   142

Red and Yellow Beets with Blue Cheese

The splendid goop that accumulates in the bottom of the salad bowl is heavenly. It's a sweet and richly sour, caramelly elixir. Just plain excellent and all it is, is pot liquor from the roasted beets, juice from the garbanzos, and balsamic melded together.

Recipe Note

Dress wedges of red and yellow beets with balsamic vinegar, pot liquor, garbanzo bean broth, coarse salt, and black pepper. Toss with wilted beet greens and garbanzos. Garnish with blue cheese.

Details

Roast the red and yellow beets in separate pans with a half inch of water or herb tea. Check your medium oven every fifteen minutes or so to turn the beets and see about adding more water. The skins will slip off pretty much once the beets are soft to the tip of a knife.

The trick here is to give the beets center stage and let the greens play a supporting role. Wilt your rustic chop of greens in a heavy pot on high heat with a little water. They'll be ready to toss with the beets in a fast minute.

Don't be shy on the pepper. There's a good reason black pepper is called the king of spices.

Plenty of blue cheese makes this salad so very creamy and satisfying.

Sweet Beets Can Replace Sugary Treats—

This heavy on the beets approach to a salad is an example of how expansive, persuasive, and satisfying the vegetable repertoire is when we use it to the full extent. If the snack train dominates your eating habits more than you'd like, try this salad. See if it doesn't help you stay on the straight and narrow. That's what our leaner French compatriots do, or at least used to do before American fast food began encroaching. They savor meals full of satisfying flavor and calories, and skip the snacks.

On Gilding the Lily with Nuts—

I often gild the lily of a salad with nuts, and hazelnuts are especially good toasted. Once removed from a 300 F oven where they've browned, their skins are relatively easy to remove by rolling the nuts between thicknesses of a large tea towel. Even the ones that the skins cling to more stubbornly than you might wish still have a great toasted flavor and plenty of crunch.

Greens with Pears and Swiss

This holiday salad serves one serious vegetable eater for lunch, two pals for a light meal, or four to six people as a dinner course. With the lettuce washed up ahead plus all manner of goodies around saying 'chose me,' it's an ultrafast fix.

Recipe Note

Dress torn lettuces and sliced shallots with good olive oil, salt, and pepper. Spritz with sherry vinegar. Toss with pears and wheat berry sprouts. (See p. 23.) Garnish with shaved Swiss cheese.

Details

I used red leaf lettuce and arugula for this particular version, although in the past I've used two varieties of lettuce from the late fall garden. One called Freckles is a light-colored loose leaf variety with inner leaves to die for.

The other was a darker endive whose name escapes me, but it had enough bitter edge to complement the mild loose leaf lettuce.

Tearing salad greens works in two ways to enhance eating enjoyment. First you get bite sized pieces that are easy for people to manage in polite company. Second, the delicate greens aren't bruised by the metal edge of your chef's knife and thus won't darken or turn bitter. That said, when I'm in a hurry, I get in there and chop lettuce with the best of them. If you're eating right away the greens will still be gorgeous.

On Dressing Salad Greens—

Years back I read that the way to truly dress salad greens is to toss them with oil first. Once that's done the vinegar or lemon juice will bead up nicely on the leaves creating just the spark you want. This thinking seems to have gone by the wayside as most recipes these days speak in terms of vinaigrettes that you mix ahead.

Still when you're not feeling lazy, you might try working the oil on first with your hands. You'll feel the greens growing buttery under your touch.

As Pacific Northwest gardening guru Steve Solomon writes in his sixth edition of *Growing Vegetables West of the Cascades*, "Nothing tastes as good as the inner leaves of a three-quarters developed, rapidly grown, tender head of loose leaf lettuce. Nothing!"

On Washing and Greens—

Washing greens isn't my favorite chore, but following Julia Child's advice makes for short work and great results. After you've picked over your greens, tossing any less than stellar ones into the compost, fill your largest mixing bowl with cold water. Plunge the greens into the bath and swish. Then transfer to a colander or loosely woven basket that allows the water to escape.

If there's no grit in the water bath as is usually the case for lettuces, you're done. Otherwise if you're working with something like muddy field spinach, change the water and repeat the routine. Even spinach is usually clean after three dunks in the drink.

On Drying Greens—

In lieu of whizzy plastic salad spinners, I layer my washed greens out on oversized tea towels. A quick roll up and then a few hours in the refrigerator drawer yields dry, crisped greens ready to dress.

I love this technique since it requires no wasting of paper towels. So it was fun to hear Lynne Rossetto Kasper, host of National Public Radio's Splendid Table, tell about how Italian country women do the same thing. Had I tapped a collective kitchen unconscious? Or had I simply done what any sensible cook would do who operates without many modern gadgets and tries to spare resources like paper towels?

On Drying Greens, Pillow Case-Style—

The problem with the system on p. 116 is that you have to plan ahead. So when friend, Sandy Kypfer, visited and I forgot to wash and dry the lettuce, she showed me a trick from her professional chef sister-in-law, Beverly Kypfer. Out came a clean pillow case and in went the washed greens.

Outside we went where I watched Sandy wind 'er up. Arms outstretched in front, gripping the case to keep it closed, she whirled it around and around. In less than a minute we were back in the kitchen ready to build a salad from perfectly dry greens.

On a Roll with Green Salads—

Making the same thing over and again is a great way to gain kitchen confidence and realize how little it takes in the way of variation to create new, interesting dishes that taste great. Salads, especially, can be great teachers.

On a second round I did the salad greens the same way, departing when it came time to garnishing. Baked, cooled butternut squash cut into bite-sized chunks and enough shaved caramelized goat cheese (Gjetost) to make people at the table want to vacation in Norway was all it took to shift gears. Once again, we ate lots of healthy vegetables even as we marveled at how delicious and beautiful our food was.

Then there was the very first time I made this salad in late fall. I used whole fresh cranberries, small Clementine oranges, and festive Stilton cheese all the way from the British Isles. The point, of course, is that most any pairing of fruit and cheese turns humble salad greens into a memorable meal.

On Winter Squash—

Winter squashes keep so well that they really know no seasonal bounds. Not only are they nigh unto essential food during the autumn and through the cold months, in June when only a single tiny crooked neck squash has appeared on out on the vine, hard shell winter squashes from last summer's season still provide fine bounty.

Busy everyday cooks really begin to appreciate winter squashes when they bake up a couple and keep them on hand in the fridge. There they become the equivalent of carrots or better, ready to add sweet heft to just about anything you're making.

On Winter Squashes and Root Vegetables—

Dark leafy greens, winter squashes, and most root vegetables tend to be omitted from our diets. Too bad since these squashes, sweet potatoes, parsnips, and their roundly rooted sisters, rutabagas and turnips, satiate like watery salad vegetables never could.

Spring Salad on a Theme of Radishes and Jicama

In the 1980s I worked at My Mom's Pie, a shag-carpeted doublewide that looked like a huge Monty Python hand had plopped it down on the Pacific Northwest coast's Long Beach Peninsula. The foggy peninsula is the same sandy spit of land that hosts The Arc restaurant so revered by James Beard, but clearly My Mom's was a different breed of cat.

But that didn't stop owner Jean McLaughlin from getting ink in Best Places *and* Sunset *magazine. She had such a touch with food and presentation, even naming the four salads she served after the earth's annual rounds well ahead of the current seasonal buzz. Indeed, McLaughlin taught me way more than the art of making pie crust. I offer this Spring Salad in her memory.*

Recipe Note

Grate radishes and peeled jicama into some fluffed spaghetti squash, and chopped spring onions. Dress with olive oil and red wine vinegar. To please the tepid and the intrepid, garnish with parsley, chile flakes, soynuts, and Parmesan.

I've long since forgotten the name of the novel, but I remember the radishes. They were prized as the earliest vegetables the spring offered, and the lead female character in the book who was of embarrassed financial circumstances wished above all other things, for fresh radishes. Oh, how she yearned for them after a long dark, winter. Crisp, crunchy, fresh radishes.

On Sweet Vegetables—

It's amazing how sweet some vegetables are. I've talked about spaghetti squash before in these pages. It's a clear winner. But jicama has been less on my radar screen until recently. What I've found is that it's light and crisp and sweet. A lovely addition whether grated or simply sliced for dipping.

On the Box Grater—

A stand-up box grater makes short work of shredding. Radishes and a host of other vegetables and fruits like jicama, carrots, rutabagas, apples and broccoli stems often get the royal treatment on my box grater. In shredded form these vegetables, peelings often included, lend an enticing persuasion to all manner of dishes. More, they are quick to cook and easy to eat.

On Fresh Parsley—

The way I've grown to appreciate a chop of fresh parsley is by the before-and-after routine. First I sit down to eat and then realize the flavor needs a boost. Often it's the missing parsley, which I confess is absent more because of laziness than amnesia. But I've learned it only takes minutes to nab a few fronds for a rinse and a chop. Back at the table, I'm thrilled by the result, as I think you will be when you go for the parsley.

Parsley grows so readily in clumps outside the kitchen door. But in the dead of winter when I buy parsley at the grocery, I store it in a jar of water in the refrigerator. With a plastic bag loosely upended over the top, the bouquet keeps way longer than if smothered away down in the vegetable drawer.

Quinoa with Peapods and Avocado

Writer and gardener pal, Laura Berg, and I have such fond memories of this salad. It was spring. We were on front patio and finished with one of our critique sessions. Life was good, and so was the food.

I included peashoots, those tender tips of the pea vines because a farmers' market vendor said the tendrils were great eating—and I had some growing along the garden fence. It's true they were fresh and fun, but they're an extra, not at all necessary for this very composed and quick salad.

Recipe Note

Into leftover quinoa, fold grated radish and finely shredded carrot along with minced parsley and mint. Dress with good oil and a light colored vinegar. Flash cook some peapods (snow peas) and cool. Use these along with peashoots and avocado wedges to garnish the quinoa. Finish with salt, pepper, and paprika.

Details

On the ratio of grain to vegetables and herbs, think tabbouleh, the renowned Middle Eastern dish. That said, know that the world's great ethnic cuisines are open to wide interpretation. Years back when I made tabbouleh with Rula Awwad-Rafferty, she had me mincing—extremely finely—way more parsley and mint than I expected.

"In Jordan it's not about the grain, it's about the greens," Awwad-Rafferty informed me with a knowing smile and toss of her lustrous dark hair.

Flash the snow peas on high heat in a splash of water for a couple minutes while their tint deepens. Err on the underdone side since they will continue to cook once out of the pan and then you can avoid the plunging in cold water step that can leach nutrients. Goal: crisp tender, bright green pods.

If you do the avocado ahead of time, paint the wedges with vinegar so they won't darken. I got fancy and used champagne vinegar. Then again, if I'd had lemons or limes in the house I'm sure I would have used them over vinegar.

Leave the salad out to come to room temperature so the flavors can blossom. Mound the doctored quinoa on a serving plate and surround with peapods. Nestle avocado and pea-shoots into the quinoa and dust with paprika, salt, and pepper.

One of the beauties of experimenting with your own amounts is that you can easily adjust depending on how many you're cooking for. In this case where I was planning lunch for two, I used a good half dozen large spoonfuls of quinoa—or enough of the cooked, chilled grain to half fill a medium sized mixing bowl. There was plenty, plus leftovers for supper.

On Quinoa—

Quinoa has become the whole grain of choice in my kitchen because it cooks quickly, tastes great, and is high in protein. I almost always have some steamed up and waiting in the fridge where it keeps a good five days.

Most say quinoa needs a rinse before cooking to remove the bitterness. I've done it both ways and can't tell the difference. Garrett Berdan, a professionally trained chef I consulted, suggested that perhaps batches of quinoa differ, some needing rinsing and others being fine as is.

What does have a pronounced, noticeable impact on quinoa is toasting before steaming it. Admittedly I don't do it all the time—or even most of the time. But when I'm in the mood for a Zen cooking moment, medium heat goes on under my cast iron wok and in goes the quinoa. Grandma's wooden spoon in my hand, schussing and brushing through the seeds. Tiny popping sounds and welcome warmth on a chilly day. The deeply satisfying smell of toasting grain. The color deepening before my eyes from a cool collected ivory to an endearing nutmeg.

Spicy Cilantro Salad with White Chocolate, Pineapple, and Cashews

It was early August and hotter than heck when the dish came to life. There was a bouquet of cilantro in the fridge along with the end of a pot of brown and wild rice. Beyond that it was all play... and play I did.

Recipe Note

Toss cilantro, minced jalapeno, chilled brown and wild rice, tofu, and fresh pineapple with good olive oil, red wine vinegar, salt, and pepper. Garnish with a toss of cashews and white chocolate chips.

On Solo Cooking—

Horse feathers to the idea that it's too much trouble cooking for one. Rather it's quite freeing since there's no one to please but mamma—or papa, as the case may be.

Indeed, I'd probably never have had the abandon to throw white chocolate chips in a salad I was making to share with another.

Details

With one grand cut, sever the thickest stems from your bunch of cilantro and give the remaining leaves and small stems a quick chop.

The jalapeno chile pepper I used was quite hot so three or four slices off the tip was plenty minced into the pile of cilantro.

I used only a couple large spoonfuls of rice which made for a very green presentation.

On the Chopping Block—

A place to slice and dice in the kitchen is paramount. Those dinky, little cutting boards that we pulled out in grandma's day were never intended for people who want to reconnect with the beauty, color, nutrition, and immense filling power of fresh seasonal vegetables. (The Mayo Clinic reports that those most successful maintaining weight eat lots of vegetables and fruits.)

Moreover, those little chopping boards never had places of honor in the kitchen where they sat out proudly at the ready. Instead they were carefully cleaned off and slipped into their slots or stored away behind the toaster.

So if you've a mind to start working with your own fresh produce, dedicate a counter top to slicing and dicing. At first it may seem like a sacrifice of precious space, but before long you'll realize—as Virginia Woolf did in, her aptly titled, *A Room of One's Own*—that your endeavors are worth it.

That's because with vegetables we're talking quantity. We need a big work surface where we can approach slicing and dicing with all the abandon of Julia Child going full bore in front of the TV cameras. We need a work surface large enough to keep at least most of the bits and shreds contained. We need room to make a great big beautiful mess!

Sweet Basil with Tomatoes and Mozzarella

Mid-July in Portland, Oregon, and my lettuce had bolted. But there it was, a single ripe tomato alongside sweet basil that was flourishing.

Recipe Note

Chop enough basil leaves to make a commodious layer of greens for a diced fresh tomato and slices from a fat round of fresh mozzarella. Finish with a minced clove of spring garlic, coarse salt, good olive oil, and black pepper.

On Sweet Basil—

Rendering sweet basil ready for the table is an art that ranges far and wide. There's chiffonading the leaves. There's rustic quick chopping. There's pounding them in a mortar with enough oil to break them down. So take your choice depending on your time and inclination. There's only one way you can go wrong with fresh basil and that's not to use it.

Thai Slaw

The thing about Thai food is that it works great in Thailand where the ingredients are fresh and affordable. So while I do splurge on Thai exotics for special occasions, most days I act like a Thai would and with a great big infectious smile just use what's around.

Recipe Note

Shred cabbage, onion, carrots, and ginger. Toss with minced garlic, a chop of fresh cilantro, dates, dried shrimp, lime juice, fish sauce, and crushed red chile. Serve the salad with garnishes of unsweetened dried coconut (toasted if you feel ambitious) and chopped peanuts.

Details

A whole cabbage, half an onion, and two carrots is a nice ratio with a small thumb of ginger and two cloves of garlic.

To be honest, I don't make slaw that much because it makes a real mess—way more so than when you are just chopping cabbage. Still, there's something about those translucent shreds of cabbage that draw you back time and again.

Instead of dates, the Thais use cane or palm sugar as the sweet element in their dishes.

Dried fruit or fruit juice, though, has the concentrated sweetness of sugar. That, plus the dimension it brings, makes it the preferred choice in my kitchen.

To grate cabbage, press a cored quarter firmly to your box grater and start shredding. You'll end up with a few outer leaves to either save for another dish or chop finely with your chef's knife.

A mortar and pestle works great to smash the garlic, chile, and ginger. Indeed, if you start exploring this approach, you'll soon be cooking like real Thai.

Tiny dried shrimp from Asian markets is pretty fishy stuff. A little is lovely. Too much, a definite dud.

If you're not in the habit of keeping cilantro around, the salad works without it of course. But like fresh parsley, cilantro makes all the difference.

What Really Happened—

Since I'm forever short of expensive limes, I used the juice from one lime and then a few shakes from a bottle of champagne vinegar. Had the fancy champagne vinegar not been around, I could have as easily grabbed any light colored vinegar or even apple cider.

You want the spice to creep up around the edges of this sweet and sour dressing. If you are new to spicy heat, try one small Thai chile, crushed or minced depending on whether you have dried or fresh. For a whole cabbage, three or four chiles pack enough zip for most American palates without overwhelming the other flavors you've developed. And yes, you can buy expensive prepared Thai chile paste, but why do that when you can develop equally fabulous flavors in your own right.

Once everything's in, it's time to fiddle. Taste with your eyes closed like in the classic film *Babette's Feast*. How's the balance between salty, sweet, sour, and spicy? If things seem bland, go for the fish sauce. If you want sweet, try more chopped dates. Same with the chile and limes, perhaps even grating some zest to throw open the door wide on fragrance of the tropics.

Fresh Ginger is Good in Moderation—

A caution with ginger is to go easy. I've found a couple thin slices are generally enough for most dishes and also that mincing it pretty fine is paramount. Biting down on a goodly sized piece of ginger when you are eating rather spoils the party. To avoid that, I sometimes grate ginger on a box grater, assured that the nice shreds will lend flavor without intruding.

Carrot Slaw with Frozen Grapes

I love one-pot, one-bowl meals, but sometimes when company comes I feel like I should make more of an effort. I'm not sure why because half the time my everyday food is better than what results when I try too hard for guests. In any event, sometimes things do work out as this simple carrot salad demonstrates.

Recipe Note

Shred carrots finely and mound on plates. Dress with fresh lime juice. Top with cottage cream (p. 20). Dust with cinnamon and garnish with chopped walnuts. Serve with frozen grapes.

Details

There's nothing like carrots grated on the fine shred. They turn into a fresh chutney-ish sort of thing, vastly different from those done on a regular grate. So when I have the time, I go for fine beguiling shred.

I keep a small dish of cinnamon on my cutting board beside the coarse salt and the red chile. That way I'm more inclined to use it than if it's all snugged up in the cupboard.

Grapes freeze right on their stems so it's an easy way of preserving them when seasonal prices have you toting home more than you can eat. Expect a sorbet experience.

Another way to love frozen grapes is pulled off their stems and doused in thick lowfat buttermilk. This is about as close to decadence as you can get without flipping over into the land of refined sugars and heavy creams. Indeed, I imagine a whirl in the blender would turn this into ice cream extraordinaire—if I can mention such things in a chapter on salads.

Main Dishes

Main dishes have almost become an oxymoron with so many fabulous soups and salads being served up for center stage. Yet, when we've time, it's nice to give a special entree top billing.

What these recipes try to do, though, is steer a course away from the standard meat (or fish) and potatoes (or rice) approach to eating. They explore dishes featuring the humble legume even as they show how eating beans does not have to mean having a dense, boring bowlful.

These recipes also investigate ethnic trends in eating, from Mediterranean to Mexican to Norwegian, with Dog Days Supper showing off a mezza platter, Juanita's Hash and Zucchini and Shrimp with Tortilla Scrolls taking us south of the border, and Brita's Salmon Cakes bringing a taste of the briny fjords.

Main dishes, of course, go well beyond the dinner table. So with a nod to being thrifty and packing your own, Lunch to Go provides a great place of departure on coming up with tasty ways to make popping the lids at lunchtime something to truly look forward to.

In sum, there are ideas for weeknights and weekends when there's more time. The range extends from shrimp and salmon to eggs and tofu and the pretty world legumes. Woven into it all are vegetables that change as the seasons make their annual rounds. The food is beautiful, and you'll feel that way too when you start conjuring in the kitchen and eating really good grub. Here's hoping!

Main Dishes

Legumes

    Dog Days Supper   148

    Hummus   149

    Lunch to Go   150

    Sou'wester Chile

        with Chocolate and Pomegranates   152

    Juanita's Mexican Hash   155

Fish

    Zucchini and Shrimp with Tortilla Scrolls   161

    Brita's Norwegian Salmon Cakes   165

    Double Treatment Salmon   168

    Mom's Favorite Dinner   173

Eggs

    Eggs with Spring Asparagus

        and Parmesiano-Reggiano   174

    Harvest Frittata   177

    Linda's Pico de Gallo   179

Dog Days Supper

When it's too hot to cook and you have August's bounty on hand, pulling together dinner is as easy as people living near the Mediterranean Sea have always known. With everything piled onto this mezza platter, all that's left to do is swab the deck, pour the wine, and nab some Greek olives.

Recipe Note

Fill a plate with tomatoes, cucumbers, chilled quinoa, and basil. Mound some hummus in the middle and raise a toast.

On Umami—

A fifth taste called umami has been identified by the Japanese and increasingly accepted by food scientists around the world. Umami refers to an overall mouth feel and exceptionally amazing deliciousness that fermented and dried foods like anchovies, fish sauce, soy sauce, vinegars, Parmesan, olives, cooked mushrooms and tomatoes, blue cheeses, wines, and liquors have. Clearly umami is a reason we so love hummus decked out with a swirl of ground, sundried tomatoes. Keep umami in mind when you're cruising in the kitchen. People won't be quite able to put their finger on it, but they'll know there's something special afoot.

"Oh," Rula Awwad-Rafferty adds as if garnishing was nothing more than a second thought in her kitchen, "decorate the hummus with a few uncrushed garbanzo beans mixed with some olive oil, lemon juice, and salt in the middle—and some reddish spice like red pepper or paprika. For the edges, perhaps a sprig of parsley or two."

"*Sahteen!* That's bon appetit in Arabic."

Hummus

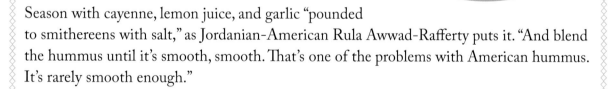

It's easy to make hummus. What you wind up with is less expensive and has way more character than store bought.

Recipe Note

Ladle out cooked garbanzos and some broth into the blender with tahini (sesame seeds ground into a butter that you can buy at the grocery).

Season with cayenne, lemon juice, and garlic "pounded to smithereens with salt," as Jordanian-American Rula Awwad-Rafferty puts it. "And blend the hummus until it's smooth, smooth. That's one of the problems with American hummus. It's rarely smooth enough."

Details

Tahini is like any nut butter, so use enough to give your hummus some backbone without getting too heavy handed.

If you think your batch of hummus still needs something after the lemon juice and cayenne, you can try my trick: a spoon of fish sauce to bring on the umami.

Lunch to Go

The best thing about this lunch to go is that it tastes as delicious as it looks. Simple colorful food. Fast to make and so fabulous to eat, the sandwich crowd will turn their heads.

Recipe Note

Layer chilled brown rice onto some baby greens in an oblong plastic container. Nestle in some baby beets and wedges of baked delicata squash. Chunks of blue cheese and a sprinkling of soy nuts round out this sumptuous feast, as does a drizzle of sesame oil, splash of vinegar, grind of pepper, and light hand with the coarse salt. A lid snaps into place, keeping things moist and delectable until midday rolls around.

Details

The secret to getting a good lunch together is having the fixin's cooked up and waiting in the fridge. A pot of whole grain. Some boiled beets. A winter squash or two. It doesn't take much.

On Special Cooking Oils—

Toasted sesame oil is my favorite and walnut oil runs a close second. They are both rather dear, but it doesn't take much of these flavorful oils to make you take notice. It goes without saying, of course, that you'd want to reserve them for drizzling over at the end where they get the attention they warrant.

On Winter Greens—

If you're just learning to speak winter greens, know that there's so much more than spinach. Kale is a favorite with me because it stays curly and green when flash cooked. It comes in several spiff varieties like lacinato (nero di toscana), Siberian, and winter red. Then again there is always Swiss chard, collards, mustard and beet greens, along with Popeye the Sailor Man's spinach. (Funny that this cartoon character's squeeze was called Olive Oil. There must have been an Italian writer in on that cartoon series when it emerged in the 1930s.)

Sou'wester Chile with Chocolate and Pomegranates

A regular Sou'wester like what they get out on the Oregon coast blew through Portland the autumn this soup came to life. The trip to the garden was a wet one, but I returned with a clutch of chard and kale. The chocolate, of course, was in the cupboard waiting— an addition inspired by mole, the Mexican sauce in which cooks take such great pride.

Recipe Note

Sauté onion, green chile, minced garlic, cinnamon, turmeric, coriander, and salt in a little oil. Add green tomatoes, cooked pinto beans, and enough bean juice and water to get a broth going. Ladle out some broth into a bowl and whisk in unsweetened cocoa powder before returning the chocolatey brew to the pot. Cut the heat; fold in a rustic chop of kale and chard. Garnish with chunks of white Cojita Mexican cheese and pomegranate seeds. Pass cruets of oil and vinegar.

Details

I froze several bags of whole green tomatoes at the end of harvest and thawed one for this chile. If you don't have green tomatoes, red that hopefully have been grown locally and sustainably would certainly fill the bill.

Intrigued by the chocolate but clueless on how much to use? Start with a couple spoonfuls and keep going until you have a velvet gravy. Add the concoction to the pot, taste, and see what you think. The idea is to simply add a little interest; a little mouth feel in the broth that will pop with the pomegranates—or some pears if they are easier the day you feel trying this out.

On Putting Food By—

If you have some freezer space you can easily put up seasonal abundance, often bagged whole with no prep at all. Whether it comes from your own garden, your membership in a consumer supported agriculture program (CSA), a farmers' market, u-pick places, or wayside stands, extra produce squirreled away can help the cause once we head into that dark, resting time of year.

On Consumer Supported Agriculture—

CSAs have helped family farms that were fading under corporate agriculture regain a footing. For a flat fee, members get regular boxes of produce throughout the growing season. It's a share-and-share-alike system. There are also annual get-togethers at the farms to help knit these burgeoning communities of producers and consumers together.

What a wonderful thing CSA's are. Children in these groups will grow up knowing where their food comes from—unlike myself who didn't consider the origins of flour until I was a young married with my first garden. There I was leaning over our porch railing and looking at the corn plants one sun-drenched day in the picturesque mining town of Jerome, Arizona, when I finally put two and two together. It was like blinders coming off.

On Pomegranate Seeds—

The only thing pomegranate seeds don't work with is salsa, beer and chips—and now that I think about it these marvelous fruits might do magical things for salsas. In any event, once the ruby red seeds are freed from their leathery husks, they do what six year old Tennessee Caitlin thinks of as a sparkle glitter hokey pokey.

Too bad that I shunned these fruits for years. That was when I thought of them as apples to be eaten in one sitting. Now that I consider them critters to be shucked and readied for all manner of tart topping, pomegranates have a revered place in my holiday kitchen.

Breaking down a half pomegranate takes only five minutes and then you have a bowl of seeds from which to draw for a couple days.

If you want to play with pomegranates, know that these jeweled fruits, as friend Dorothy Read calls them, grace us only briefly each year. By January they are a fading memory.

Juanita's Mexican Hash

It was back in the late-1960s in Northern Arizona when I met Juanita Baca, a round grandmother who wore plaid housedresses and sweaters. Her adobe home was spotless, and her cast iron cook stove did double duty, simmering pots of frijoles and warming her long, narrow back room.

Juanita knew all about living close to the seasons, from the green chile that she put up for winter to the hash she made midsummer when the tomatoes and winter squashes were small and green.

Recipe Note

Brown onion and garlic in oil with a chop of last year's green chile from the freezer. Use small pours of water to keep things moist while the onions sweat. Add diced green tomatoes and green squash from the garden. Cover on low heat until the squash is meltingly sweet. Serve on platters topped with grated cheddar and nicely chopped cilantro. Round out the meal with warm corn tortillas and bowls of chile beans.

Proper Mexican madré that Juanita was, she put in a year's supply of green chile each fall. Home her husband, Ramon, would come from taking the healing waters in New Mexico, gunny sacks of chile in tow. Into action Juanita went, roasting, peeling, and freezing her treasure of chile.

The dry crystalline snow of the Colorado Plateau may have piled up in frigid mounds outside the door, but around Juanita's table there was plenty of heat from chile she fried with potatoes, posole, and just about everything in between.

On Red and Green Chile—

Treatises have been written on the world of red and green chile. It puts the zing in Thai food, keeps us coming back for Mexican food, and is always at the ready near my chopping board. At least the dried red pods are.

My green chile—both Anaheims and jalapenos—is frozen away in small bags just like Juanita used to do. I put it up at summer's end, first roasting the pods in the oven and then removing the pith and most of the seeds that if left would make the heat overpowering.

Most cooks take the skins off as well, but I'm not picky. Some slip off and that's great, but for the ones that are clingy, what the heck. Besides, when I lived in Hopiland, we always at the skins on our green chile. The cook would bring a platter to the breakfast table, and the rest was up to us. We'd pull the hot core end out and the rest we'd savor with eggs and potatoes.

These days, I like to unfreeze some green to spice up a pan of squash or pot of whole grains. Still, my faithful standby is red chile—whether from the petite ristra I strung with tiny fish peppers I grew last summer or store bought.

Dried red is handy, even though some foodies say green has the real flavor. It makes sense that fresh is best, but in the winter if there's no green in sight you can count on red. Sometimes I crush a bit of red chile into a mince of garlic and serve it on a condiment plate of its own, a maneuver that's a hit since people at the table can control their own levels of these high power items.

On a Roll with Crook Neck Hash—

Truth be told, when I made this hash last year it departed significantly from Juanita Baca's version. Yet I held fast to her theory and used what was available in the garden. I did gather some green tomatoes along with a few small green chile peppers including a jalapeno, but instead of sacrificing early winter squashes I found a few yellow crook necks that were fairly ripe. Also alongside some lush sweet basil, my scraggly cilantro looked decidedly unappetizing. Guess which one garnished the hash.

On Legumes—

Canned beans are quite the racket, me thinks. One can costs about as much as a pound of dry beans and who knows how much of the nutrition was leached out in the processing. Besides, it's so easy to put a pot of beans on the back burner to simmer.

I buy organic beans in twenty-five pound bags. If you figure around a pound of beans for a small pot, that's a fair amount of highly affordable protein not to mention a stash on hand in the event of emergency.

There is no substitute for home cooked legumes. Not only do you wind up with the most wonderful syrupy broth, you also get people walking into your house saying, "Smells good in here!"

A pound of legumes is about two cups. I do four to five cups at a time in our old orange Le Crueset pot. The heavy enameled cast iron keeps the beans from burning on the bottom. To get legumes ready to cook, pour them into something with plenty of room like a large basket so you can pick out any stray pebbles and then give them a rinse.

There are various theories out there on the benefits of soaking legumes. Who knows which are right, but it does make sense that less cooking fuel is needed when the beans have softened in cold water ahead of time.

On the digestion problems that have so maligned the worthy legume, *Cook's Illustrated* experimented and found that bringing a pot of beans to a one minute boil, soaking for an hour before draining and then cooking in fresh water reduced the flatulence-producing properties of legumes by 43 percent. This method surpassed soaking beans overnight which showed only a 28 percent reduction. That said, *Cook's* noted that the quick soak adversely affected the texture of the beans and thus was not their preferred choice.

Mexican food guru Rick Bayless maintains that eating beans often is the only way to resolve digestion problems. Perhaps that's the case, although I also wonder if serving size doesn't figure in as well. Small amounts of legumes in dishes that include other sources of protein seem to pose few if any problems for most people. Peruse French or Italian cookbooks, and you'll find beans often included in recipes as one of many ingredients.

I rarely add so much as an onion and salt to legumes which makes putting a pot on the stove a something I can do in five minutes while talking on the phone. After the fact, as small amounts of beans get incorporated into various dishes, they pick up plenty of flavor making fussing ahead of the curve academic. Then again, sometimes when I feel like it I'll fiddle a bit. Onions, garlic, salt, red or green chile, maybe even a couple spoons of oil into the pot when I put the beans on.

Cooking times vary depending on the legume. While garbanzos, or chick peas as they are also called, can take a good half day to cook into delectable tidbits, most other legumes like pinto beans just need a couple hours on the burner. It's so very homey to smell a pot of legumes cooking in your kitchen on wintry weekends—and all they ask for is plenty of water and low heat.

My system on managing freshly cooked legumes is to freeze all except what I'll be using over the next few days. With a large pot this works out to a nice covered bowl in the fridge plus half a dozen cartons in the freezer, each in their own syrupy juice.

Zucchini and Shrimp with Tortilla Scrolls

After some blistering midsummer weather, Portlanders were graced with a week of cloudy skies complete with rain. It was still too hot to want soup, but this one pot dish hit the spot. It was also a delicious way to celebrate a gift of a dozen zucchinis.

Recipe Note

Flash cook zucchinis, red peppers and minced garlic on high heat in a little water until the vegetables are crisp tender. Add the shrimp and leave over the heat until just pink. Season with salt and pepper.

Toss with fresh spinach and cilantro. Drizzle with good olive oil. Garnish with lemon and orange wedges. Serve with warm corn tortillas rolled into yellow scrolls.

Details

What dictated the number of zucchini I used in this dish was what was in the fridge. In that respect, I was in illustrious company.

"I had many, many lunches with Julia Child over the years. She always made omelets and we'd have a glass of wine—sometimes two," K. Dun Gifford, founder of Oldways a food issues think tank, told me in an interview with an arch of his confident Bostonian brow. "It was always the same. She'd go to the refrigerator and say, 'Dun, dear, what shall it be? Shrimp? Scallions?' I'd always answer, 'Oh, whatever's in there that needs using, Julia.'"

Vegetables cooked just to crisp tender keep their color, vibrancy and taste.

Overcooked vegetables boiled "beyond the point at which they can do no harm," in humorist Garrison Keillor's words, may not be as bad as dumping in a can of cream of mushroom soup, but they come darn close.

On a Roll—

Round 1—**Tomatoes and Fresh Mozzarella**-We had leftovers but they didn't linger. When yet another mealtime rolled around, the zucchini, greens, and shrimp morphed into a composed salad with the addition of fresh tomatoes, basil, and chunks of fresh mozzarella. Dressed with oil and vinegar, and salt and pepper, this dish practically made itself.

Round 2—**Crook Neck Squash, Shallots and Polenta**-When you get on a roll and make variations of a dish over and again, as some ingredients get used up others take their place. In this case crooked necks in the garden were itching for a chance to bid those visitor zucchinis good by. It was the same with the shrimp. They were long gone and a carton of pinto beans thawed from the freezer clamored for their moment, so away we went.

I flash cooked the yellow squash with a small bell pepper, pith and seeds removed. The vegetables started sticking to the pan, and I doused them with more water than I'd intended. But it turned out okay since the cooked pintos weren't very soupy and needed the juice.

Also once the vegetables were tender—and here's where it got fun—I sprinkled in a little polenta right from the sack. It absorbed the excess liquid, leaving behind all vestiges of a soup and creating a stewy, meaty dish that accommodated a topping of grated cheddar.

There you have it. The kitchen goddesses were smiling, as I've found they do so often for cooks willing to get in there with a whole lot of pluck.

Pastry Scrapers Do Double Duty—

With its rounded handle and straight rectangular blade, this five by four inch piece of stainless steel makes transferring chopped vegetables from the cutting board to the pan easy. These inexpensive tools run under eight dollars and pay off handsomely—particularly if you situate your chopping surface handy to your stove so that the transfer ends up being a heave ho operation punctuated by little more than a step or two.

Brita's Norwegian Salmon Cakes

This is my paternal grandmother's recipe, although as she half apologetically said, it isn't really a recipe since there aren't any measurements. The story goes that Brita Bjornevald Johnson was a stubborn Norwegian if there ever was one, but she sure could cook as these salmon cakes abundantly demonstrate. They have no starchy filler or eggs and are light and tender.

Recipe Note

"Bone and skin a fresh salmon and put the flesh through a meat grinder twice. Don't use more than two or three pounds of fish to try out since it accumulates a lot during the making."

"Then beat it for a while, using a big bowl and wooden spoon. Start diluting it with milk, a little at a time until it gets like thick mush."

"Season it with salt and nutmeg. It takes quite a lot of nutmeg, about a tablespoon for two pounds of fish."

"Beat it some more, and as it gets thicker add a little more milk all the while pulling out any of the tiny white membranes you see. Be sure to add the milk sparingly, because too much makes the cakes flat when you fry them."

"Try a dab on the frying pan first using a spoon dipped in cold water. If your cake puffs up and looks fluffy, you got a good do and can start cooking. Brown the cakes slightly in a little oil and then put them to stay warm and moist in a pan with a little fish broth… Here's hoping!"

Details

The first time I made these I was uncertain even though I'd seen my grandmother and mother make the delicacies many times. But the tiny Norske lady's "here's hoping…" seemed such a cordial invitation.

Filleting and grinding the fish was straightforward, and I remembered to not scrape the grinder too scrupulously, thus leaving the bulk of the stringy white membranes caught in the works of the machinery. As for the few membranes that got through, it was just a matter of picking them out with a fork while I was beating the milk in for the thick pudding.

Boiling the carcass in enough water to strain off a cup or two of broth was easy too; basically like making tea. Finally frying the salmon cakes in a skillet filmed in oil was akin to doing pancakes, so no problem there.

These days, I often do the cakes without messing with a whole salmon, using a chunk of fillet from a butcher that sells wild fish. While there are no bones for the broth, there's still the skin with the goodly amount of flesh that adheres to it after cutting the fillet away. Then again, a vegetable broth of carrot, onion, fennel, and parsley is a venerable option as well.

Double Treatment Salmon

Broiling after baking turns the pink flesh of the salmon a tantalizing golden brown. Dotting the fillet with garlic butter doesn't hurt the cause either.

Recipe Note

Encase a wild salmon fillet in a foil tent and leave fifteen minutes in a medium hot oven. Pull away the top layer of foil to expose the fish. Sprinkle on dill, paprika, salt, and pepper. Dot with garlic butter and run under the broiler until gorgeous.

Details

Tear off a long sheet of aluminum foil. Put the fish on one end and bring the rest over the top, folding and crimping the sides to seal the fish in its tent. If you want to spare the foil, use a covered roasting pan or casserole dish.

For garlic butter, put a pinch of coarse salt on your cutting board, mince three or four cloves of garlic into the salt, and work the mince into a soft cube of butter. This will leave lots of extra garlic butter for putting on vegetables, frying up some Spanish rice, and what have you.

Leave the oven door open when you're broiling. This salmon doesn't take but a couple minutes to turn the color of a Arizona sunset.

If you make this during September, check out Linda's Pico de Gallo (p. 179) for an accompaniment. Or if it's spring, try some flash cooked asparagus and quinoa along side the fish.

On Carnivores and Vegetarians—

It's true. Since we Americans speak meat and potatoes so very well, this book focuses mostly on vegetables, whole grains, and legumes. I'm in good company as no less a mainstream organization as the Humane Society of the United States advocates a vegetarian diet on behalf of freeing factory farm animals from the abuse many currently experience.

And then, of course, there's Michael Pollan's *Omnivore's Dilemma* and Ann Vileisis' new book, *Kitchen Literacy,* not to mention my friend Marsha's reaction to the stockyards she drove by on a California road trip. "I really wish I hadn't seen it. It was wretched. The poor cows crowded in on each other, and it was grossly unsanitary." I related Marsha's tale to a mutual friend, Gary, and his observation was that he heard it's equally as sickening with mass production of chickens. "We just don't eat any of that," he said about he and his wife's dietary preferences.

Sometimes I wonder about eating wild fish as well and do try to avoid the species with high mercury levels. But, my father fished for salmon on the Oregon coast after he retired, and my grandfather newly immigrated from Norway in the early 1900s harvested oyster beds for years from one of the Pacific Northwest's generous bays. So what can I say about eating the occasional piece of wild fish other than, "Ya, sure. You betcha."

On Wild Salmon v. Farm Fish—

All manner of weird things go on when fish are penned up as farm animals. They get diseases and need antibiotics. What's in their feed can make you shudder. They don't get exercise so their flesh is flaccid and so pale that marketers dye it. Besides all that, think of the impoverishment of living in pens when your forbears made magnificent anadromous journeys from river to sea over hundreds of fathomless miles. Clearly wild salmon are more expensive than farm fish. A trick here is to save on a few meals by eating legumes. That will free up extra funds for consumers who want to buy food with integrity—and participate in what Alice Waters calls "the delicious revolution."

Watermelon Postscript—

We stood at the edge of the deck to finish this meal. There we were with cold slices of red melon, spitting our seeds out into eternity.

Mom's Favorite Dinner

I've always found it interesting that my meat-eating mother's favorite dinner was nothing but three vegetables: tomatoes, green beans and corn. For sure the meal was served with chicken or some type of meat, but that wasn't what got the attention. Rather it was the trio of vegetables from her Iowa childhood that she loved so.

Recipe Note

Slice fat home grown tomatoes crosswise into thick slabs. Flash the beans on high in a heavy skillet with enough water to keep them moist while their color deepens slightly and they turn crisp tender. Boil shucked roasting ears and get the butter and bibs ready.

I see this meal fleshed out with some Dover sole, that delicate white fish my mother so loved. Also some garlic bread made from 100 percent whole grain flour.

To do the bread, spread with garlic butter (p. 168), wrap the slices in a foil tent, and warm in a medium oven until piping hot.

(It's nice to leave the extra slices of bread wrapped in the foil so they'll stay hot for those who want seconds.)

Eggs with Spring Asparagus and Parmigiano-Reggiano

This really is one of the very best ways I've had asparagus. And such a quick fix. The trick is to make it during the spring when asparagus enjoys prime time.

Recipe Note

Snap the ends off your asparagus and flash cook it. Fry an egg sunnyside up. Shave on some first class Parmigiano-Reggiano right from the Italian bergs that gave the world this cheese, and go to feasting.

Details

Use just enough water when you're flashing the asparagus to keep it from burning. Ideally the spears will be tender and still bright green just as the last of the water evaporates.

If you flash the asparagus in a skillet, you can use the same pan to do your eggs. Get the heat just right here—closer to medium. And use a lid to help cook the egg without having to turn it. That way there will be just the right amount of runny yolk to sauce your plate.

If you're feeling ambitious, slivered garlic crisped in the oil before frying the eggs makes for an exceptional garnish.

On Dressing Asparagus—

Edouard de Pomiane, the cook Elizabeth David so revered, explains in his book, *Cooking with Pomiane*, that butter by itself "doesn't stick to the asparagus sufficiently [and is] to be honest, a little disappointing." Short of a full-blown hollandaise, he reports that sieved, hard-cooked egg yolks stirred into melted butter do yeoman service on behalf of asparagus.

No wonder I love this dish so. Simply frying an egg gets Pomiane's requisite components on the plate in a manner that's close enough for the guys I go with.

And it's done in minutes.

Harvest Frittata with Roasted Peppers and Summer Squash

Frittatas, those eggy Italian approaches to light suppers, brunches, and appetizers are everyone's friend since they're easy as pie. Frittatas are really just scrambled eggs with a lioness's share of vegetables and enough cheese to melt your heart.

Recipe Note

Whisk some eggs with a spoonful of milk or water, cottage cheese, salt, and pepper. Add a chop of roasted sweet peppers and summer squash. Pour into a heavy oiled skillet and cook on medium without stirring. Once the eggs are mostly set, grate some Asiago over the top with pinches of paprika and nutmeg. Run under the broiler to finish the eggs and melt the cheese. Serve with Linda's Pico de Gallo (p. 179).

Details

I had leftover roasted summer squash and peppers the day I made this particular frittata, so in they went. Also I wanted extra protein and put a few generous spoons of cottage cheese into the mix. The white curds showed prettily when we were eating.

It's easy to figure out how many eggs to use by how many you're feeding, of course. Plus, since wedges of frittatas are so excellent that they use them for starters in Italy, there's no need to worry about leftovers.

Use medium heat and enough oil to film the surface of a skillet that will go from the stove top to the broiler to the table. Let the pan come up to temperature before pouring in the eggs and cook them until they are mostly set—sometimes a lid helps here if you have an extra thick frittata.

Most any vegetables work in frittatas. In fact, I'd wager that if we looked into the history of this dish, we'd find it originated with everyday cooks coming up with a way to use leftover vegetables. Fresh vegetables like spinach and mushrooms can work as well, although if you don't want to bother with flash cooking them separately, they'll take a smaller chop so they soften nicely as the eggs cook.

Linda's Pico de Gallo

Linda Thompson's life has been steeped in the Southwest. Her father was a mule skinner on the Bright Angel Trail in the Grand Canyon, and over the years her mother, Eagle, acquired an impressive collection of silver and turquoise jewelry.

Eagle also owned the Coffee Pot Café in the railroad town of Williams, Arizona, fifty miles south of the canyon. Both mother and daughter, though, have culinary skills that extend considerably beyond meatloaf and cherry pie, as is clear from this pico de gallo Linda made when she visited with her youngest son, Raymond Wesley.

Recipe Note

Thompson started with a small dice of tomatoes from my garden that she said "made this salsa."

Then she added "fresh garlic, jalapenos—one or two depending on how hot you want it—and a couple fresh green chiles with the skin on. Sometimes I will add a yellow pepper or two for color and taste. There are so many wonderful varieties of hot to mild peppers, although I don't care for the poblano chile in this."

The chiles and garlic, of course, were chopped finely to match the tomatoes. Then came "sea salt, diced onion, fresh cilantro," said Thompson, cautioning that too much cilantro can overwhelm the other flavors.

To finish, all she did was load up on the lime juice.

"Juice from freshly squeezed from limes is essential," she emphasized, an exquisite Navajo bracelet of heavy silver encircling her wrist as she sliced the citrus. "About two for every three cups of this fresh salsa."

On the Chef's Knife—

The chef's knife has a wide blade so you can use a rocking motion when chopping, mincing, and slicing. Trying to accomplish these maneuvers with another type of knife is one reason people have reduced themselves to buying things like bagged greens. More's the pity, as Midwesterners say, since it really is a matter of getting the right tool for the job.

On the price of the knife, stay true to your budget. Grocery stores have cheap chef's knives for as little as fifteen dollars. I own one of these, and it has provided faithful service over many years even if the blade is rarely as sharp as I'd like. There are the high-carbon stainless steel forged knives that run between seventy-five and a hundred dollars as well. When you pick up one of these stout babies, you know you have a fine tool in your hand. Also, they hold an edge far longer than the cheapies or the mid-priced stamped knives.

Endings

"We always had dessert after dinner," said my aunt, Kirsten Wilson. "Even if it was just canned peaches."

Amen to that. But then my aunt came from a staunch Norwegian background where the habit was to move from the table into the living room with the java and take some convivial leisure around a large, deeply polished coffee table.

Wherever and however you have dessert, the recipes offered here revolve largely around fruit, cheese, and a bit of chocolate. Also with the exception of a store-bought gourmet cookie, they steer clear of sugar.

But that doesn't mean there isn't sweetness. Check out the stuffed dates for ideas on how to run a serious race with Snickers bars. Or the Chocolate Goodies for a truly unique way to offer chocolate.

During the colder times of the year, there are two ideas for using sweet, sweet pears. And come summer, there are Blue Moon Apricots, one of those dishes that once you try it will most likely become an annual tradition.

Cheeses, of course, are welcome any time. Those last rich morsels that bring a satisfying ending to a meal. Ahh....

Endings

Blue Moon Apricots   186

Cheese Plates   187

Baked Pears with Caramelized Goat Cheese   189

Gorgonzola with White Chocolate Chip Cookie   191

Brie and Coconut   192

Allspiced Pears and Clementine Oranges   193

Stuffed Dates   194

Chocolate Goodies   196

Blue Moon Apricots

First honors go to Blue Moon Apricots. Those who follow my blog might remember this great finish. It came on a whim one July evening when apricots were in season and I'd left some blue cheese out. As Olive Blackwell, longtime family friend who was over, said, "They tasted just as yummy as they look."

Recipe Note

Split and pit perfectly ripe apricots and arrange on a common plate. Put a nugget of blue cheese in the center of each half. There's no need for dessert plates and forks. This is finger food all the way.

Details

The first key to this dessert is using soft, plush apricots picked at the height of the season. The second is to have your cheese room temperature. No doubt about it, cheese turns into a different critter altogether when it has a chance to warm up after being refrigerated. An hour or two is a conservative estimate of time cheese can sit out safely.

Cheese Plates

Europeans are known for finishing their meals with cheeses and perhaps some fruit. Rather a nice way to distance oneself from sugary confections and so very simple.

Recipe Note

Set two or three wedges of cheese out on a board either with or without pieces of fresh, seasonal fruit.

On Cheese—

Christmas Eve last year after a Pacific Northwest Dungeness crab feed, I served caramelized goat cheese with persimmons, fruit you can only get during the holidays. Like Goldilocks said, "It was *just* right."

Often I go for blue cheeses with their tangy, disarming notes. While artisan domestic producers are making first rate varieties, they aren't cheap. Then again, if you compare the price to ice cream…

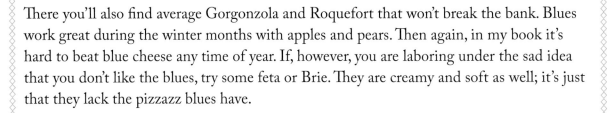

If you're new to the world of cheeses beyond longhorn—or even cheese not sliced up by some big machine some-where—check out the deli cheese case at the supermarket for the reasonably priced Danish blue.

There you'll also find average Gorgonzola and Roquefort that won't break the bank. Blues work great during the winter months with apples and pears. Then again, in my book it's hard to beat blue cheese any time of year. If, however, you are laboring under the sad idea that you don't like the blues, try some feta or Brie. They are creamy and soft as well; it's just that they lack the pizzazz blues have.

When you want to serve several cheeses make each choice distinctive. Perhaps a domestic blue cheese or chèvre produced in your area and a round of Smoked Edam or Gouda. Keep in mind too, that a chunk of Parmigiano-Reggiano, or its cousins Asiago or Romano, also works on cheese plates with its salty sour assertiveness. We tend to think of the Parmesan family for grating only, when this fabulous group of cheeses is good for nibbling.

Baked Pears
with Caramelized Goat Cheese and Lime

On a stormy March night when you're wishing the weather was already a lamb, these warm limey creations keep the lions at bay.

Recipe Note

Core d'Anjou pears and sit in a little water or port wine. Bake until soft to the tip of a knife. Stuff with caramelized goat cheese and put back in the oven for a few minutes. Serve with lime wedges. Garnish with lime zest and freshly grated nutmeg.

Details

D'anjou pears hold their shape well during baking. While ones that aren't entirely ripe will bake, they won't soften as nicely as pears that truly are ready to eat.

In a medium oven, pears usually take a half hour or more. The idea with the water is to have enough to keep the juice that escapes while the fruit bakes from burning. It doesn't take much.

I like caramelized goat cheese (Gjetost) here but it any number of cheeses that melt nicely, from Brie to fontina to Gruyère, would work nicely.

Sometimes I'll skip the cheese and use cottage cream (p. 20), but that isn't the only way to make your baked pears dressy-uppy. There's always plain yogurt or sour cream.

Fresh lime juice accents the pears like a booming drum roll. And if you feel like picking up the microplane, some zest over the top signals all that it's a limey kind of night.

On a Roll with Baked Pears—

I also like to bake pears with a little ruby port poured into the cavities and pan. You end up with some exceedingly divine goop for spooning over, and there's no need for cheese at all.

Another approach to doing pears is to bake them whole and split them once they're done. With a rest on your cutting board, they cool enough for you to core them.

This is a nice approach when your pears are large, and you want to serve just a half to each person.

Gorgonzola with White Chocolate Chip Cookie Wedges

Neighbors Ryan Wayman and Patrick Earnest still wax more eloquently than you'd believe about this dessert. It was one of those spur of the moment things where scarcity forces your hand. I had a single gourmet cookie and three yearning for a decadent ending to a meal.

Recipe Note

Cut a big soft cookie into sixths and arrange the pie shaped pieces around room temperature Gorgonzola. Serve with a couple butter knives so people can nudge bits of cheese onto their pieces of cookie while they enjoy their after dinner coffee.

Brie and Coconut

So simple and elegant, yet this white on tan ending doesn't need to be pretentious.

Recipe Note

Serve a wedge of Brie on a bed of toasted unsweetened coconut.

Details

Unsweetened coconut is available in bulk bins at whole foods stores and many mainstream grocers. Toast it on medium heat in a heavy pan. A few minutes of careful stirring will net fragrant, tawny shreds that are so seductive people won't miss the sugar we've come to associate with shredded coconut.

An ending like this is easy to manage away from the table, so it's nice to move into the living room around the coffee table like my cousins in Tertnes, Norway—the Askeland family—do.

Allspiced Pears and Clementine Oranges

Here's a holiday offering that is, like little girls, full of spice and everything nice.

Recipe Note

Dip chunks of pear painted with lemon juice and Clementine orange segments halfway into melted butter and then into flax meal spiked with freshly ground allspice. Arrange on small trays with stuffed dates, pecans, and pomegranate seeds for parties, friends, the postal carrier, and the man who picks up the recycling and garbage.

Details

No offense to Mr. Bartlett, but enough already. So feel free. Bring home a variety of pears and see which ones get your attention.

Stuffed Dates

The only problem with stuffed dates is that they're so good people with a sweet tooth can overdo.

Recipe Note

Pit Mejol dates and stuff with blue cheese.

Details

Better grocers carry big boxes of fat fresh Mejol dates during the holidays. It's worth it to see where you can find these since last year's Mejols that sit around in bulk bins get worse for the wear.

To pit a date make a lengthwise slit on one side.

On a Roll with Stuffed Dates—

The variations here are almost endless:
- Press a pecan half into the cheese.
- Roll the stuffed date in powdered sugar.
- Fill dates with crème fraîche, sour cream, hummus, or cream cheese whipped with a little milk to make it spreadable.
- Use a chèvre or caramelized goat cheese (Gjetost) instead of blue cheese.

- Stuff dates with nut butters ground from almonds, cashews, or peanuts.
- Dip one end of a stuffed date in some melted butter and freshly ground cardamom.
- Or do like Carole Branom says her cousin Art McCray does. "Tuck a tiny sliver of jalapeno into a cheese stuffed date."

Chocolate Goodies

We tend to assume that chocolate is nowheresville without sugar, but these goodies demonstrate otherwise. Check them out in the photo out on the chapter frontispiece, p. 183.

Recipe Note

Grind raisins and walnuts. Work in enough unsweetened cocoa to make a dough that holds together without being too sticky. Press the dough out into a thick round the diameter of your hand and decorate with finely chopped walnuts.

Details

Get out grandma's old meat grinder for this one. The raisins and walnuts will turn into a thick paste. Then wash your hands and plunge in, working as much cocoa powder into the mix as it will take.

Once you have a nicely blended dough, flatten it out into a circle on a buttered plate. Chop a few more walnuts for scattering on top to make things look pretty. To make the walnuts stick nicely, press them into the dough with a rolling pin.

"It was so good," said my pastry chef neighbor, Meredith Cairns about the chocolate goody I took over. "I'll have to get the recipe. What'd you put in it, some kind of fruit?"

Meredith was right. The fruit is raisins. Yet just as with the adage, "it's not what you do but how you do it," these goodies pop not so much from the raisins themselves, but the way they're handled. Being game to get out the old meat grinder is all it takes.

Index

A

Alfalfa Seeds 23
Allspiced Pears and Clementine Oranges 193
Almonds
    Spiced Turnips and Cardamom Almonds 67
Amaranth 19
    Figgy Cereal 18
Apples 25, 188
    Apples with Beanpaste, Kasha, and Lime 32
    KBJ's Cranberries 36
Apricots
    Blue Moon Apricots 186
Asparagus
    Eggs with Spring Asparagus
        and Parmigiano-Reggiano 174
    Roasted Asparagus and Garlic Shoots 71
Avocado 49
    Quinoa Salad with Peapods and Avocado 131

B

Baked Pears with
    Caramelized Goat Cheese and Lime 189
Basil, Sweet [140, 149, 155
    Clifford's Mary Pesto 63
    Snap Beans with Pesto 60
    Sweet Basil with Tomatoes and Mozzarella 138
    On Sweet Basil 138
Beanpaste 39
    Apples with Beanpaste, Kasha, and Lime 32

Beanpaste 33
Beans. *See* Legumes
Beets
    Beets with Chives 82
    Lunch to Go 150
    Red and Yellow Beets with Blue Cheese 116
    Sweet Beets Can Replace Sugary Treats 118
Black Pepper 116
Blue Moon Apricots 186
Bob's Polenta Waffles 42
Brie and Coconut 192
Brita's Norwegian Salmon Cakes 165
Broccoli 128
Brown Rice 19, 39, 106
    Lunch to Go 150
Buckwheat 32
Buttermilk 86, 143

C

Cabbage
    Soupy Soup with Cauliflower and Limas 100
    Thai Slaw 139
Capsicum Quotient 68
Caramelized Onions, Oven-Style 78
Carrots
    Carrot Salad with Frozen Grapes 142
    Roasted Parsnips and Carrots 69
Cashews 195
    Cashew Cilantro Pesto 75
    Quinoa with Raspberries and Cashews 22
    Spicy Cilantro Salad with White Chocolate
        Chips,
        Pineapple, and Cashews 134
Cast Iron 60, 72, 78

On the Griddle 40
Cauliflower
 Soupy Soup with Cauliflower and Limas 100
Cereal
 Apples with Beanpaste, Kasha, and Lime 32
 Figgy Cereal 18
 Fruit and Dip 28
 Pulled Strawberries 30
 Quinoa with Raspberries and Cashews 22
 Swiss Birkermuesli 29
Cheese
 Asiago 177, 188
 Blue 116, 148, 150, 186, 188, 194
 Brie 188, 192
 Caramelized Goat Cheese (Gjetost) 25, 124, 194
 Cheddar 48
 Chèvre 188, 194
 Cojita 152
 Cream Cheese 49, 194
 Feta 188
 Fontina 189
 Gorgonzola 188, 191
 Gouda 188
 Gruyère 189
 Longhorn 188
 Mascarpone 85
 Mozzarella 138, 163
 Parmesan 63, 96
  Parmigiano-Reggiano 174
 Pepper Jack 44
 Romano 188
 Roquefort 188
 Smoked Edam 188
 Stilton 124
 Swiss 120
 Baked Pears with Caramelized Goat Cheese 189
 Blue Moon Apricots 186
 Brie and Coconut 192
 Cheese Plates 187
 Cheesy Corn Bake 53
 Corncakes with Pepper Jack 44
 Egg and Cheese Tacos 48
 **Eggs with Spring Asparagus
     and Parmigiano-Reggiano 174**
 **Gorgonzola with White Chocolate Chip
     Cookie Wedges 191**
 Greens with Pears and Swiss 120
 Quinoa Logs 25
 Red and Yellow Beets with Blue Cheese 116
 Sweet Basil with Tomatoes and Mozzarella 138
 On Caramelized Goat Cheese 26
Chile
 Fried Red Chile, Hopi-Style 81
 **Sou'wester Chile
     with Chocolate and Pomegranates 152**
 Capsicum Quotient 68
 On Red and Green Chile 156
 On Roasting Green Chile 54
Chocolate
 Chocolate Goodies 196
 **Sou'wester Chile with Chocolate
     and Pomegranates 152**
 **Spicy Cilantro Salad with White Chocolate Chips,
     Pineapple, and Cashews 134**
Chowder
 **Salmon Chowder with Roasted Tomatoes and
     Sweet Peppers 108**
 On Chowders for the Gang 110

Chutneys 28, 142
Cilantro
    Cashew Cilantro Pesto 75
    Delicata Squash with Cashew Cilantro Pesto 74
    Spicy Cilantro Salad with White Chocolate,
        Pineapple, and Cashews 134
Clifford's Marvy Pesto 63
Coconut 105, 139, 192
Cooking Oils
  On Fats and Cooking Oils 47
  On Fats in Our Diets 82
  On Special Cooking Oils 151
Cooks and Chefs
  Awwad-Rafferty, Rula 65, 131, 148-49
  Baca, Juanita 155, 157
  Bayless, Rick 159
  Beard, James 127
  Berdan, Garrett 133
  Berg, Laura 109
  Branom, Carole 61
  Branom, Jessie 72
  Cairns, Meredith 196
  Child, Julia 101, 136
  David, Elizabeth 82, 85, 175
  Del Rio, Dulce 23
  Farmer, Fannie 12
      Fannie Farmer Cookbook 9
  Flicker, Doug 111
  Goforth, Bob 42
  Goforth, Bob and Beth 64
  Jenkins, Steve 26
  Johnson, Brita (Grandma) 105, 133, 165
  Johnson, Kathleen Brown (Mom) 36, 38, 72
  Kypfer, Beverly 124

Kypfer, Sandy 124
Lowman, Bunny 71
McCray, Art 195
McLaughlin, Jean
    My Mom's Pie 127
Peynaud, Lulu 101
de Pomiane, Edouard 85, 175
Punlert, Daeng Arporn 12, 65, 92
Tawayesva, Joyce 32
Thompson, Linda 179
Waters, Alice 13, 171
Wilson, Kirsten (Aunt) 39, 184
Corn
    Mom's Favorite Dinner 173
Cornmeal
    Bob's Golden Polenta Waffles 42
    Cheesy Cornbake 53
    Corncakes with Pepper Jack 44
  On Cooking Polenta 43
  On Polenta and Cornmeal 43
Corn Tortillas 155, 161
    Egg and Cheese Tacos 48
    Zucchini and Shrimp with Tortilla Scrolls 161
Cottage Cream 18, 28, 32, 35, 142, 190
    Cottage Cream 20
Cranberries 34, 124
    KBJ's Cranberries 36
  On a Roll with Cranberries 36
Cream 85
Cucumbers 106, 148
    Cucumber-Melon Soup 105
  On a Roll with Cucumber Soup 106

Cultural References
  Asian 84, 93
  Askeland Family, Tertnes, Norway 192
  Awwad-Rafferty, Rula 65, 131-32, 149
    "*Sahteen!* That's bon appetit in Arabic" 148
  Baca, Juanita 155, 157
  British Isles 124
  Hopi 32, 40, 43, 54, 68, 81, 156
  Hungary 70
  Johnson, Brita 165
  Johnson, Rognald and Brita 26
  Jordan 132, 149
  Mediterranean 148
  Mexican 152, 155
  Middle East 131
  Navajo 43, 180
  Norwegians 108
  de Pomiane
      Polish 85
  Punlert, Daeng Arporn
    Bangkok, Thailand 12, 65, 92
  Ruiz, Germán
    Puebla, Mexico 11
  Spaniards 70
  Tawayesva, Joyce and Clark
    Sipaulovi, Arizona, Hopiland 32
  Thai 68, 92, 95, 139, 156

D

Dates 29, 139, 141
  Stuffed Dates 194
Delicata Squash
      with Cashew Cilantro Pesto 74
Dog Days Supper 148

Double Treatment Salmon 168

E

Eclectic References
  Arizona sunset 169
  Babette's Feast 141
  Celebrating a Moment with Fresh Garlic 77
  Coffee Pot Café, Williams, Arizona 179
  Colorado Plateau 64, 155
  Dylan, Bob 50
  Gifford, K. Dun 162
  "Go Directly to Lunch" card 64
  Goldilocks 187
  Jerome, Arizona 154
  Keillor, Garrison 162
  Latin Jazz
    Gary and Argelis Lewis 25
  Monty Python 127
  Mortensen, Chad and Meredith Cairns
    Oregon's wine country and u-pick orchards 18
  Northern Arizona 64
  Old MacDonald's Farm 50
  Popeye the Sailor Man and Olive Oil 148
  Raggedy Ann 30
  Soupy 100
  Armies that were down to nothing but legumes… 22
  Zen cooking moment 133
Ecological References
  Eddings, Larry 31
  Here a Chick, There a Chick 50
  Humane Society of the United States 50
  Making Sense of Egg Labels 52
  On Strawberry Fields Forever? 30
  On Wild Salmon v. Farm Fish 171

Rollan, Bernard 50
Shaprio, Paul 52
Edouard's Mother's Tomatoes 85
Eggs
    Cheesy Corn Bake 53
    Egg and Cheese Tacos 48
    Eggs with Spring Asparagus
       and Parmigiano-Reggiano 174
    Harvest Frittata 177
    Ben and Jerry's 50
    Here a Chick, There a Chick 50
    Humane Society of the United States 50
    Making Sense of Egg Labels 52
    On Eggs and Omelets, Fluffy, Rich
       and Otherwise 49
Equipment
    Blenders 20
    Grinder 165-67, 196
    Measuring tools, lack of, pre-1900s 8
    On the Box Grater 128
    On the Chef's Knife 181
    On the Chopping Block 136
    On the Griddle 40
    Pastry Scrapers Do Double Duty 164

F

Fats
    On Fats and Cooking Oils 47
    On Fats in Our Diets 82
Figs
    Figgy Cereal 18
Fish Sauce 110
    On Fish Sauce 95
    Salt and Pepper v. Fish Sauce and Chile 95

Flax meal 18, 25, 29, 193
Fried Red Chile, Hopi-Style 81
Fruit and Dip 28

G

Garlic 149, 174
    Roasted Garlic 76
    Breathe Deep the Gathering Aromatics 103
    Celebrating a Moment with Fresh Garlic 77
    Postscript on Roasted Garlic 77
Garlic Bread 173
Garlic Butter 168
Garlic Shoots
    Roasted Asparagus and Garlic Shoots 71
Ginger
    Breathe Deep the Gathering Aromatics 103
    Fresh Ginger is Good in Moderation 141
Gjetost. *See* Cheese, Caramelized Goat Cheese
Gorgonzola with White Chocolate Chip
      Cookie Wedges 191
Grapes
    Carrot Slaw with Frozen Grapes 142
Green Beans. *See* Snap Beans
Greens
    Baby 150
    Beet greens 116, 152
    Collards 152
    Kale 152
    Mustard 152
    Spinach 49, 152
    Swiss Chard 152
    Greens with Pears and Swiss 120
    Lunch to Go 150
    On Dressing Salad Greens 121

On Drying Greens 122
On Drying Greens, Pillow Case-Style 124
On Washing Greens 122
On Winter Greens 152

H

Harvest Frittata
      with Roasted Peppers and Summer Squash 177
Hazelnuts
    On Gilding the Lily with Nuts 119
Health, Weight, and Purse Strings
   Bircher-Benner, Maximillian, MD 29
   economy in trouble 9
   Fast, Julie 10
   food bills rising 9
   Mayo Clinic 136
   obesity and overweight epidemic 9
   On Carnivores and Vegetarians 170
   On Fats and Cooking Oils 47
   On Fats in Our Diets 82
   On Sugar Sensitivity 25
   On Whole Grains and Food Dollars 19
   ready-to-eat food 9
   Seibert, Karen, MS 25
   Sweet Beets Can Replace Sugary Treats 118
   Weil, Andrew, MD 18
   vegetable peelings 69
Herbs
   Mint 131
   On Fresh Herbs 109
   On Fresh Parsley 129
Hot and Sour Shrimp Soup,
      Thai-Style 92
Hummus 33, 78, 194

Dog Days Supper 148
Hummus 149

J

Jicama
   Spring Salad on a
        Theme of Radishes and Jicama 127
   On Sweet Vegetables 128
Juanita's Mexican Hash 155

K

Kale 84, 96, 152
Kasha 19
  Apples with Beanpaste, Kasha, and Lime 32
KBJ's Cranberries 36
Ketchup, homemade 70
Kitchen Thoughts
   Breathe Deep the Gathering Aromatics 103
   Celebrating a Moment with Fresh Garlic 77
   equivalent of a small chemistry experiment 10
   Get Thyself a Smashing Device 65
   health and wealth 9
   It's All in What You Have on Hand 75
   kitchen goddesses 163
   Millet's not Just for the Birds 98
   On the Artistry of Cooking 111
   On Carnivores and Vegetarians 170
   On the Chopping Block 136
   On Consumer Supported Agriculture 153
   On Cooking with Wine 99
   On Cruising with Some Zip 102
   On Gilding the Lily with Nuts 119
   On Learning Curves 40
   On Leeks and Less Familiar Vegetables 97

On Making Things Ahead 21
On Putting Food By 153
On Solo Cooking 134
On Soup Stock 101
On Sweet Vegetables 128
On Umami 148
On Vinegared Milk, Buttermilk, Yogurt, and Beer 46
On Whole Grains and Food Dollars 19
quick-fix convenience 62
Plain Jane Cooking 22
no more small chemistry experiment 10
too tired, too busy to cook 10
Watermelon Postscript 171
What Really Happened 141
Kiwi 18

L

Leeks
  On Leeks and Less Familiar Vegetables 97
Legumes
  black beans 94
  garbanzos (chickpeas) 33, 94, 116, 149
  limas 94
  mung beans 23
  pintos 94, 163
  white beans 33
  Apples with Beanpaste, Kasha, and Lime 32
  Beanpaste 33
  Hummus 149
  Juanita's Mexican Hash 155
  Soupy Soup with Cauliflower and Limas 100
Sou'wester Green Chile 152
Lemons
     On Lemon Juice and Sours 111

Apples with Beanpaste, Kasha, and Lime 32
Linda's Pico de Gallo 179
Literary and Scholarly References
  Ashby, LeRoy 8
  Belasco, Warren
    Appetite for Change 39
  Best Places 127
  Bittman, Mark
    New York Times 19
  Child, Julia
    The Way to Cook 13, 101
  Cooks Illustrated 159
  de Pomiane, Edouard
    Cooking with Pomiane 175
  Farmer, Fannie
    Fannie Farmer Cookbook 9
  Gifford, K. Dun 162
  Hughes, Holly
    Best Food Writing (2005) 111
  Laurel's Kitchen 102
  Kalpakian, Laura
    American Cookery: A Novel 30
  Olney, Richard 101, 111
    Lulu's Provencal Table 11
    On the Artistry of Cooking 111
  Parsons, Russ
    How to Pick a Peach 35
  Pollan, Michael
    Omnivore's Dilemma 170
  Rollan, Bernard 50
  Shapiro, Laura
    Julia Child 58
    Perfection Salad 9
  Solomon, Steve

Growing Vegetables West of the Cascades 121
Sunset Magazine 127
Vileisis, Ann
    Kitchen Literacy 170
Woolf, Virginia
    A Room of One's Own 136
Lunch to Go 150

M

Markets, Farms, and Grocers
    Bob's Red Mill 43
    On Consumer Supported Agriculture 153
    New Seasons 26
    Rose City Park Presbyterian Church
        Hollywood Farmers' Market gleanings 74
Measure free cooking philosophy and history 8-13
  Fast, Julie 10
  Olney, Richard 11
    On the Artistry of Cooking 111
  Ruiz, Germán 11
Melon 171
    Cucumber-Melon Soup 105
Millet 19, 39
    Minestrone with Millet 96
    Millet's Not Just for the Birds 98
Mortar and Pestle
  Get Thyself a Smashing Device 65
Mushrooms 178
Mustard Seeds
  On Cruising with Some Zip 102

N

Nuts
  On Gilding the Lily with Nuts 119

O

Olives 148
Onions
    Caramelized Onions, Oven-Style 78
    Breathe Deep the Gathering Aromatics 103
Oranges
    Allspiced Pears and Clementine Oranges 193
    KBJ's Cranberries 36
    Thanksgiving Breakfast 34

P

Pancakes and Waffles
    Bob's Polenta Waffles 42
    Corncakes with Pepper Jack 44
    Rolled Up Pancakes 38
Paprika
  On Paprika 70
Parsley
  On Fresh Parsley 129
Parsnips
    Roasted Parsnips and Carrots 69
Peapods
    Quinoa with Peapods and Avocado 131
Pears
    Allspiced Pears and Clementine Oranges 193
    Baked Pears with Caramelized Goat Cheese and
        Lime 189
    Greens with Pears and Swiss 120
    On a Roll with Baked Pears 190
Peppers
    Salmon Chowder with Roasted Tomatoes and
        Sweet Peppers 108
Persimmons 187

Pesto
  Cashew Cilantro Pesto 75
  Clifford's Marvy Pesto 63
  Delicata Squash with Cashew Cilantro Pesto 74
  Snap Beans with Pesto 60
  Postscript on Pesto 64
Pineapple
  **Spicy Cilantro Salad with White Chocolate,
    Pineapple, and Cashews 134**
Polenta 155
  Bob's Polenta Waffles 42
  On Cooking Polenta 43
  On Polenta and Cornmeal 43
Pomegranates
  **Sou'wester Chile
    with Chocolate and Pomegranates 152**
  On Pomegranate Seeds 154
Potatoes 110, 170
Pulled Strawberries 30

Q

Quinoa 19, 39, 46, 161
  Dog Days Supper 148
  Quinoa Logs 25
  Quinoa with Peapods and Avocado 131
  Quinoa with Raspberries and Cashews 22
  On Quinoa 133

R

Radishes
  **Spring Salad on a
    Theme of Radishes and Jicama 127**
Raisins 29, 196
Raspberries

  Quinoa with Raspberries and Cashews 22
Red and Yellow Beets with Blue Cheese 116
Relish 78
Roasted Vegetables
  Caramelized Onions, Oven- Style 78
  Roasted Asparagus and Garlic Shoots 71
  Roasted Garlic 76
  Roasted Parsnips and Carrots 69
  Snap Beans with Pesto 60
  Spiced Turnips and Cardamom Almonds 67
  On Roasting Vegetables 72
  Wintertime Roasts 61
Rolled Up Pancakes 38
Rutabagas 76, 125

S

Salmon
  Double Treatment Salmon 168
  **Salmon Chowder with Roasted Tomatoes and
    Sweet Peppers 108**
  On Wild Salmon v. Farm Fish 171
Salsa 96
  Linda's Pico de Gallo 179
Salt
  On Coarse Salt 70
  Salt and Pepper v. Fish Sauce and Chile 95
Shrimp
  dried 139-40
  **Hot and Sour Shrimp Soup,
    Thai-Style 92**
  Shrimp Cups 84
  Zucchini and Shrimp with Tortilla Scrolls 161

Snap Beans
    Mom's Favorite Dinner 173
    Snap Beans with Pesto 60
    To Stem Snap Beans or Not 61
    Wintertime Roasts 61
On Soup Stock 101
Soupy Soup with Cauliflower and Limas 100
Sour Cream 20, 190
**Sou'wester Chile
       with Chocolate and Pomegranates 152**
Soy Nuts 150
Spices
    Allspiced Pears with Clementine Oranges 193
    Spiced Turnips and Cardamom Almonds 67
    Fresh Ginger is Good in Moderation 141
    On Grinding Your Own Spices 62
    On Paprika 70
    On Turmeric 102
Spinach. *See* Greens
**Spicy Cilantro Salad with White Chocolate,
       Pineapple, and Cashews 134**
Spring Salad on a Theme of Radishes and Jicama 127
Sprouts 22
    On Sprouting Grain, Seeds, and Beans 23
Squash
    Butternut 21, 124
    Crook Neck 157, 163
    Delicata 150
    Spaghetti Squash 46, 84, 127
    Zucchini 53
    **Delicata Squash
       with Cashew Cilantro Pesto 74**
    **Harvest Frittata with Roasted Peppers
       and Summer Squash 177**

Juanita's Mexican Hash 155
Lunch to Go 150
Zucchini and Shrimp with Tortilla Scrolls 161
    On a Roll with Crook Neck Hash 157
    On Sweet Vegetables 128
    On Winter Squash 125
    On Winter Squashes and Root Vegetables 125
Strawberries 28
    Pulled Strawberries 30
    On Strawberry Fields Forever? 30
Stuffed Dates 194
Sugar
    On Sugar Sensitivity 25
Sweet Basil with Tomatoes and Mozzarella 138
Sweet Potatoes
    Thanksgiving Breakfast 34
    On Sweet Potatoes or Yams 35
Swiss Birkermuesli 29

T

Tahini 149
Tempeh 94
Thai Slaw 139
Thanksgiving Breakfast 34
Tofu 42, 75, 94, 134
Tomatoes
    Dog Days Supper 148
    Edouard's Mother's Tomatoes 85
    Linda's Pico de Gallo 179
    Mom's Favorite Dinner 173
    **Salmon Chowder with Roasted Tomatoes
       and Sweet Peppers 108**
    Sweet Basil with Tomatoes and Mozzarella 138

Turmeric
   On Turmeric 102
Turnips
   Spiced Turnips and Cardamom Almonds 67

U

Umami
   On Umami 148

V

Vinegar
   On Lemon Juice and Sours 111
   On Vinegared Milk, Buttermilk,
   Yogurt, and Beer 46

W

Waffles
   Bob's Polenta Waffles 42
Walnuts 29, 63, 98, 142, 196
Wheat Berries 22
Whipped Cream 34
   On a Roll with Whipped Cream 35
Whole Grains
   Apples with Beanpaste, Kasha, and Lime 33
   Figgy Cereal 18
   Quinoa with Raspberries and Cashews 22
   Rolled Up Pancakes 38
   Swiss Birkermuesli 29
   Quinoa with Peapods and Avocado 131
   Millet's Not Just for the Birds 98

   On Sprouting Grain, Seeds, and Beans 23
   On Whole Grains and Food Dollars 19
Wine and Liquor 190
   On Cooking with Wine 99

Y

Yogurt 20, 190

Z

Zucchini 53
   Cheesy Corn Bake 53
   Zucchini and Shrimp with Tortilla Scrolls 161

Jean Johnson is a food writer and holds a doctorate in cultural history. She lives in Portland, Oregon where she reads, writes, bikes, cooks, and gardens.